PREFACE

WATER is essential to life. On, in and around our ponds and streams, a multitude of living things are to be found. Many are invisible without a microscope, but there are also a great number which can be seen with the naked eye. Among the plants are some which are beautiful though inconspicuous, others which may be a nuisance to oarsmen and fishermen, and still others which have a part to play in forming the soil on which we live. Some of the animals are a source of livelihood to Man, but both these and the many others deserve — and repay — careful study for their own sakes. And in undertaking such a study, much the best way is to see the creatures in their natural surroundings.

In the compilation of this book a great many species have had to be collected and identified; we hope that it will enable its users, likewise, to identify the plants and animals they find, as the essential preliminary to a more detailed study and record of the organisms.

Although our aim has been to make the book unusually comprehensive for its size, it has been necessary to omit a number of species: we trust that our choice may nevertheless meet with approval. We should welcome any suggestions and criticisms from our readers.

In the task of adapting the book to the needs of naturalists in Britain, Miss Mona C. Harrison has kindly co-operated with me. I thank her most heartily for her work in translating the text, adding fresh details and attending to it in other ways. I should like further to express my thanks to the artists, L.P. Pouderoyen and Jos Ruting, and also to the publishers of the Dutch edition for allowing this edition to appear.

W. J. Prud'homme van Reine

Zaandam (The Netherlands)

May 1957

v

NOTE ON TERMINOLOGY

English names are given, where they exist, for each species, followed by the scientific names in Latin. The abbreviations at the end of some of the latter refer to the biologist to whom the name is attributed. Brackets round some of these indicate that the name has been changed by modern authors. When a second Latin name is given it is because both are still in general use.

A Glossary of biological terms used in this book is to be found on pages 150 to 152.

Plants and Animals of Pond and Stream

A HANDY GUIDE CONTAINING DRAWINGS AND
DESCRIPTIONS OF OVER 500 SPECIES OF PLANTS,
INSECTS, FISH, BIRDS, ETC.

Willem Jeremias
W. J. Prud'homme van Reine

ref from
REINE

Translated from the Dutch and adapted for use in
Great Britain in collaboration with **Mona C. Harrison**

Illustrated by **L. P. Pouderoyen** and **Jos Ruting**

John Murray Albemarle Street London

1957/68

First published in Great Britain 1957
Reprinted 1968

Printed by The Ysel Press, Deventer, Holland
and published by John Murray (Publishers) Ltd.

CONTENTS

PLANTS

The vegetation found in and beside fresh water is very extensive and very varied. This is not surprising, as water is so important a substance to the life of a plant. Water contains dissolved mineral salts, oxygen and carbon dioxide, all indispensable to the plant. Plants actually growing in water are largely supported by it and so do not have to develop the strengthening tissues found in land plants. Roots may be practically non-existent and only develop when needed to fix the plant in a definite place.

Scientists have good grounds for believing that the earliest plants existed only in the water. They were not 'plants' in the ordinary sense, but unicellular organisms of microscopic size. We do not know exactly what they were like but biologists have some idea from remains found in soil layers of great antiquity.

It is not possible here to consider the way in which modern plants have evolved from the early forms. However, some water plants have characteristics which show that they have evolved from land plants. The original water plants gave rise to land plants, but from these some water plants have again been evolved. That such an evolution is possible, can be seen by considering plants growing on the banks of ponds and streams where they are frequently exposed to flooding.

When plants die in the winter, the dead plant-remains fall to the bottom of the water and gradually decay, though not as rapidly as do plants on land; thus the bottom layer becomes thicker and the water becomes shallower.

As a stream becomes shallow, the Bulrushes and Reed-maces are able to grow, soon followed by the reeds. Later come the Water Parsnip, Sweet Flag and Water Dock, all growing on the bank and raising the soil, so that, after a time, dry land comes into existence.

The first land formed in this way is boggy, and there one can find the Marsh Marigold, Bog Forget-me-not and Cuckoo Flower.

If these plants are left undisturbed, Willows, Alders and Birches soon grow to form a small wood. The soil, consisting mainly of peat, will lack sufficient mineral salts and oxygen and the plants will not grow strongly. Gradually the ground becomes more acid as more plants decay; the fen may be filled with Bog Moss and the vegetation supplanted but more soil is formed. Thus we get a higher bogland, where Sundew, Butterwort and eventually Heather grow. Good examples of this are found in the Lake District and in Ireland.

In this book plants which live in the water and along the banks have been listed, but most of the bog plants have been omitted.

A point of detail that may be mentioned here is that plants which have their roots in the mud at the bottom of a pond or stream soon suffer from a shortage of oxygen. To prevent this there are large air-canals leading from the leaves to the roots. As the leaves grow above the water, these canals are in contact with the air through the stomates.

A. MOSSES *(Musci)*

1. **Bog Moss**—*Sphagnum sp.*

    Stem upright; the lower leaves decay and the upper part grows increasingly higher. The leaves have no mid-rib and contain two different kinds of cells. There are many species of *Sphagnum*; the one in the drawing is *Sphagnum squarrosum Pers.*

    The Bog Moss retains large amounts of water and is therefore used to pack the roots of plants when they are dispatched from nurseries.

2. **Water Moss** - *Fontinalis antipyretica Hedw.*

    Best known as an aquarium plant. Stem much branched. Leaves arranged in three distinct rows, folded and curved. 1 foot.

    ('1 foot' means that the stem reaches 1 foot in height).

3. **Brook Moss**—*Leptodictyum riparium Warnst.*
    Stem branched. Leaves less obviously in three rows; green
    and very transparent. Pointed leaf-tips, distinct mid-ribs.
    Older parts usually brown.
    On the roots of trees and on stones near water. 2-3 inches.

4. **Wall Moss**—*Rhynchostegium murale B.S.G.*
    Stem partly creeping. Leaves concave with pointed tips,
    clearly serrated near the tip.
    On rocks and trees near the water's edge. 3 inches.

5. **Bank Moss**—*Homalothecium sericeum B.S.G.*
    Stem creeping, strongly branched. Leaves folded long-
    itudinally (plicate) with a distinct mid-rib, the edge usually
    entire.
    Turf-like, at the water's edge. 6 inches.

    Scorpidium scorpioides Limpr.
    Sturdy, bronze-green moss in boggy places. Leaves curved
    to one side, appearing claw-like.

    Drepranocladus lycopodioides Warnst.
    Like the previous one, but the leaves are pointed and have a
    mid-rib.

B. LIVERWORTS *(Hepaticae)*

6. *Ricciella sp.*
    A liverwort. Narrow, flat, branched stems, found floating
    on the water.

C. CLUBMOSSES *(Lycopodiales)*

7. **Quillwort**—*Isoetes lacustris L.*
    Rather stiff, dark green, spiky leaves. Spore-cases in the
    wider part of the leaf. The spores have nodules on them.
    Locally abundant. 4 inches—1½ feet.

Isoetes echinospora Dur.

Rather flaccid, light green, narrow, spiky leaves. The spores have long spines.

Local. (*Isoetes tenella Lem.*) 2—8 inches.

D. HORSETAILS *(Equisetales)*

8. **Water Horsetail**— *Equisetum fluviatile L.*

Stem about $\frac{1}{3}$ inch thick, smooth with fine lines. Sheaths with 10-12 black, triangular teeth with membranous edges. Common in bogs and ditches. *(Equisetum limosum L.)* 4 feet.

Marsh Horsetail— *Equisetum palustre L.*

Stem up to $\frac{1}{4}$ inch thick, grooved. Sheaths with 6—10 teeth with broad, white membranous edges.

Common in moist places.

E. FERNS *(Filicales)*

9. **Pillwort**—*Pilularia globulifera L.*

Creeping stem, with erect bristle-like leaves. The young leaves arising in a coil like a spring; as in all Ferns. The pods of the spore-cases are the size of a pea, brown-black in colour.

Rather rare. On the margins of ponds and lakes, may be abundant in favourable situations. Leaves up to 6 inches long.

10. *Salvinia natans All.*

There are three leaves at each node of the small, sometimes branched, stem. Two of the leaves are floating, oval and usually have heart-shaped bases. The third is finely divided and performs the functions of roots. Between these "roots" are the spore-cases in bulbous pods.

Not found wild in Great Britain. 3 inches.

11. **Water "Fern"**—*Azolla filiculoides Lam.*

Stem much branched with deeply bi-lobed leaves. In sunny places it is reddish-brown coloured. Sometimes it covers

4

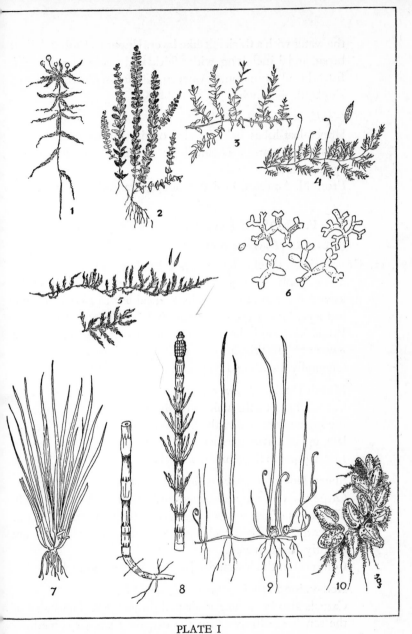

PLATE I

1. Bog Moss; 2. Water Moss; 3. Brook Moss; 4. Wall Moss; 5. Bank Moss; 6. *Ricciella*;
7. Quillwort 8. Water Horsetail; 9. Pillwort; 10. *Salvinia natans*.

the water with a thick felt-like layer. Upper leaf-lobes $\frac{1}{10}$ inch broad and $\frac{1}{12}$ inch long, with a fairly wide, colourless margin. Introduced from South America. Naturalised in the south of England. $\pm \frac{3}{4}$ inch.

Azolla caroliniana Willd.
Upper leaf-lobes half the size of the former species. The colourless margin is small or missing; not completely symmetrical.
From N. America. Probably not naturalised. $\pm \frac{1}{2}$ inch.

F. FLOWERING PLANTS *(Angiospermae)*

(i) DOCKS *(Polygonaceae)*

12. **Great Water Dock**—*Rumex hydrolapathum Huds.*
Stem deeply grooved and slightly branched. Large, entire leaves; one leaf at each node. Radical leaves 2—3 feet long, leathery. Lower leaves are mostly heart-shaped at the base. Petals surround the fruit (an important characteristic of *Rumex sp.*) In this one each fruit has a tubercle.
Generally distributed. July and August. $\pm$ 5 feet.

Marsh Dock—*Rumex palustris Sm.*
Carpels have teeth, which are shorter than, or as long as, the segments and have thick tubercles. Radical leaves lanceolate, upper leaves narrow.
Local. June to September. 40 inches.

Sharp Dock—*Rumex conglomeratus Murr.*
Carpels have a tongue-shaped projection on the tip of each. The stalks of the sepals which cover the fruit are as long as the carpels. Each carpel has a tubercle. Radical leaves are slightly heart-shaped.
Common in the lowlands. June to August. 40 inches.

Red-veined Dock—*Rumex sanguineus L.*
Carpels also have tongue-shaped projections. The stalks of the sepals are longer than the carpels. One, or sometimes

6

three, of the carpels have a tubercle. Flowering stems have leaves only at the base.
Common in the South. June and July. 4 feet.

13. **Amphibious Bistort**—*Polygonum amphibium L.*
Creeping rootstock, with ascending stems, numerous and unbranched. Leaves lanceolate, short stalked. When growing in the water the leaves have long stalks. Flowers pink or white, in a dense spike. Two kinds of flowers, namely:—flowers with long styles and short stamens and those with short styles and long stamens.
June to October. 40 inches.

Spotted Persicaria—*Polygonum persicaria L.*
Stem has a filmy sheath, with a toothed edge, above each node. Leaves having each a darker fleck. Flowers pink, in dense spikes.
Common. June to October. 40 inches.

Soft Persicaria—*Polygonum mite Schr.*
Stem has a filmy sheath, with large teeth, above each node. Leaves lanceolate. Flowers red or white, more scattered along the stem. Fruit $\frac{1}{10}$ inch across.
Local, mostly in the south. July to October. ± 1 foot.

Slender Persicaria—*Polygonum minus Huds.*
Stem with filmy sheaths, having a few, short teeth. Leaves mostly narrow. Fruit $\frac{1}{12}$ inch across.
Local, throughout Britain. July to October. ± 8 inches.

14. **Water-pepper**—*Polygonum hydropiper L.*
Stem branched. Leaves lanceolate, the upper ones small, with a strong peppery taste. Flowers green at the bottom, the tips white to red, scattered along the stem.
Common. July to October. ± 16 inches.

7

15. **Water Blinks**—*Montia lamprosperma Cham.*

Stems floating in masses, of which many are without flowers. Leaves spatulate; edge entire, arranged in opposite pairs. Flowers white, two large and three small petals.
Rather rare. In brooks. May to September. 1 foot.
(Montia fontana L.) (Montia rivularis C. C. Gmel.)

(iii) **STARWORTS** *(Callitrichaceae)*

16. **Autumnal Starwort**—*Callitriche hermaphroditica L.*

Stem thread-like. Leaves arranged crosswise, narrow with a broader base and distinct mid-rib; dark green. Flowers without bracts. Fruits winged, a keel on the upper side. The whole plant is submerged.
July to October. 10 inches.
(Callitriche autumnalis L.)

17. **Bog Starwort**—*Callitriche stagnalis Scop.*

Stem thread-like. Obovate leaves, arranged crosswise. Flowers with sickle-shaped bracts. Styles persistent. Fruits winged, somewhat divergent, with a keel on the upper side. In water or boggy places. May to October. 10 inches.

18. **Spring Starwort**—*Callitriche palustris L.*

Stem thread-like. Leaves arranged crosswise, lower ones narrow, upper ones obovate. Bracts present. Fruits narrowly winged, with keel. Upper leaves sometimes floating. Also found in bogs. Rare. April to July. 10 inches.
(Callitriche verna L.)

Callitriche intermedia G. F. Hoffm.
Stem thread-like. Leaves crosswise, obovate. Styles hook-shaped, falling early. Fruits not winged, often keeled.
In water. April to October. 10 inches.
(Callitriche hamulata Kütz)

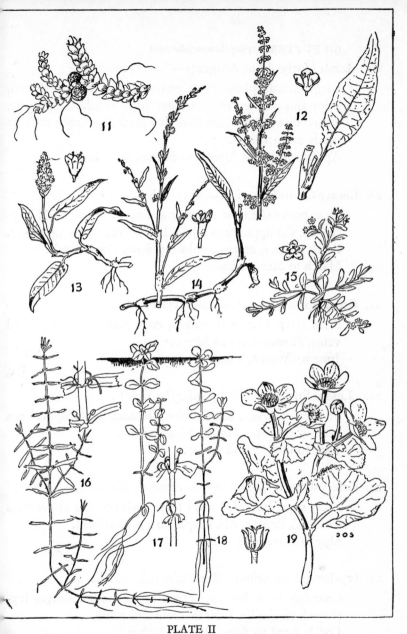

PLATE II

11. Water "Fern"; 12. Great Water Dock; 13. Amphibious Bistort; 14. Water-pepper;
15. Water Blinks; 16. Autumnal Starwort; 17. Bog Starwort; 18. Spring Starwort;
19. Marsh Marigold or Kingcup.

19. **Marsh Marigold or Kingcup**—*Caltha palustris L.*

Large, sturdy plant. Stem branched, leaves heart-shaped, shiny and dark green; short stalked or sessile. Large, fine, yellow flowers. Flowers have five petal-like sepals; the true petals are nectaries.

April to May and August to September. 1 foot.

20. **Lesser Celandine**—*Ranunculus ficaria L.*

Stem procumbent or ascending. Leaves heart- or kidney-shaped, the upper ones lobed. In the lower axils are tubers. Petals oblong, narrow, golden-yellow. Three sepals.

March to May. 10 inches.

21. **Great Spearwort**—*Ranunculus lingua L.*

Stem erect. Leaves lanceolate, edge entire, almost parallel veins. Flowers over an inch across.

June to August. 4 feet.

21a. **Lesser Spearwort**—*Ranunculus flammula L.*

Stem erect. Lower leaves oblong-lanceolate, the upper ones narrower. Flowers up to ½ inch across.

June to October. 18 inches.

22. **Celery-leaved Crowfoot**—*Ranunculus sceleratus L.*

Erect stem. hollow. Lower leaves palmate, the upper ones tri-lobed. Small petals. Carpels in a conical head.

May to November. 2 feet.

23. **Ivy-leaved Crowfoot**—*Ranunculus hederaceus L.*

Creeping stem, hollow, rooted at the nodes. Leaves ivy-shaped, all similar. Flowers small and white.

Local. April to September. 10 inches.

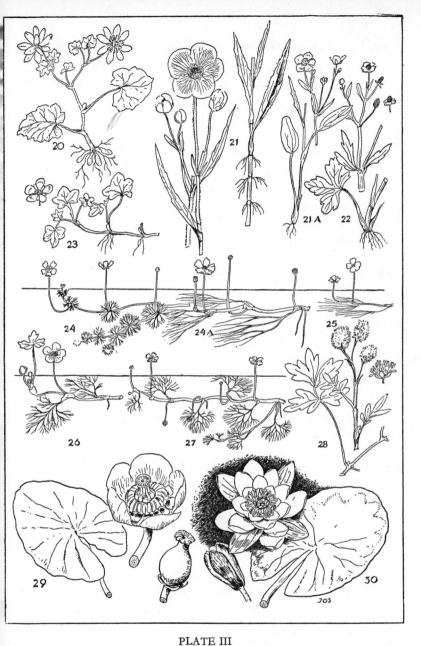

PLATE III

20. Lesser Celandine; 21. Great Spearwort; 21a. Lesser Spearwort; 22. Celery-leaved Crowfoot; 23. Ivy-leaved Crowfoot; 24. Circular-leaved Crowfoot; 24a. River Crowfoot; 25. White Water Crowfoot; 26. Water Crowfoot; 27. Dark Hair Crowfoot; 28. Common Madow Rue; 29. Yellow Water Lily; 30. White Water Lily.

24. Circular-leaved Crowfoot—*Ranunculus circinatus Sibth.*

Stem floating, submerged leaves divided into many rigid segments, which remain stiff when the plant is taken out of water. All leaves submerged.
Locally common. June to August. 40 inches.

24a. River Crowfoot—*Ranunculus fluitans Lam.*

Segments of the submerged leaves are very elongated, lying parallel in the water. Lower leaves long-stalked; upper ones sessile. 5 to 12 petals.
In streams and rivers from the Clyde southwards. June to August. 20 feet.

25. White Water Crowfoot—*Ranunculus ololeucos Ldloy*

Submerged leaves divided into long, thin segments, floating leaves tri-lobed. Nearly all the leaves have stipules, the uppermost are the largest. Flowers about $1\frac{1}{2}$ inches across.
Not known in Great Britain. May to July. 2 feet.

26. Water Crowfoot—*Ranunculus aquatilis L.*

Similar to no. 25 but stipules of the upper leaves are attached halfway or higher on the petioles.
April to August. 10 feet.

27. Dark Hair Crowfoot—*Ranunculus trichophyllus Chaix.*

Floating leaves, if present, are tri-lobed. Small leaves. Under 20 stamens.
May to August. $6\frac{1}{2}$ feet.

28. Common Meadow Rue—*Thalictrum flavum L.*

Stem erect, grooved. Leaves two or three times pinnate, the leaflets are mostly palmati-partite with three lobes. The lower leaves have stipules. Flowers yellowish, fragrant.
June and July. 3 feet.

29. **Yellow Water Lily or Brandy Bottle**—*Nuphar lutea Sm.*
Petioles triangular (this is not clear in the drawing) with large air-spaces. Leaves floating, heart-shaped with deep basal lobes. Five yellow sepals, small yellow petals.
May to August.

30. **White Water Lily**—*Nymphaea alba L.*
Petioles cylindrical with four large air-spaces (not clear in the drawing). Leaves floating, round with a heart-shaped base. Four outer green sepals and many white petals.
May to August.

(vi) **HORNWORTS** *(Ceratophyllaceae)*

31. **Hornwort**—*Ceratophyllum submersum L.*
Floats freely. Leaves three-forked, in whorls. Segments sparsely toothed. Fruits without spines. Plant light green.
Mainly in the S.E. June and July. 2 feet.

31a. **Prickly Hornwort**—*Ceratophyllum demersum L.*
Floats freely. Leaves once or twice forked, in whorls. Segments stiff and closely toothed. Fruits with two spines at the base. Dark green.

(vii) **CRESSES** *(Cruciferae)*

32. **Great Yellow Cress**—*Rorippa amphibia Besser*
Stem somewhat creeping, branched. Leaves of the water-form are slightly emarginate; the land-form are deeply incised. Petals bright yellow. Fruit a siliqua, longer than the style but much shorter than the fruit stalk.
Locally common, mostly in the north. May and June. 3 feet.

Marsh Yellow Cress—*Rorippa islandica Borbas*
Stem ascending, branched; sometimes procumbent. Leave deeply divided, particularly the lower ones. Leaf segment

toothed. Petals pale yellow. Fruit an oblong siliqua, about the same length as the stalk.

In water or boggy places. June to September. 16 inches.

33. **Common Water Cress**—*Nasturtium officinale R.Br.*

Stem ascending, hollow and angular. Leaves pinnate, leaflets elliptical. Fruit a siliqua, somewhat curved, about as long as the stalk ($\pm \frac{1}{12}$ inch long).

In or near water. Common. May to October. 4 inches to 2 feet.

(viii) WATERWORTS *(Elatinaceae)*

34. **Waterwort**—*Elatine hydropiper L.*

Stem creeping. Leaves spoon-shaped, petiole usually longer than the leaf-blade. Flowers sessile, in leaf-axils. Four petals, eight stamens. Fruit with horseshoe-shaped seeds. On the bank. Rare and local. July to August. 6 inches.

Six-stamened Waterwort—*Elatine hexandra D.C.*
Creeping stem. Elliptical leaves. Stalked flowers. Three petals and six stamens.
On the bank. Very rare. July to September. 4 inches.

(ix) *(Rosaceae)*

35. **Meadow Sweet**—*Filipendula ulmaria Maxim.*

Stem bulbous, underground. Leaves pinnate, with alternating small and large, serrated leaflets and a large, palmate, terminal leaflet; the upper surfaces green, the lower ones covered with hairs. (Sometimes both surfaces are green). Large stipules. Flowers yellowish-white in close clusters.

June to August. 2 to 4 feet.

36. **Marsh Cinquefoil**—*Potentilla palustris Scop.*

Stem branched, ascending. Leaves compound with three to seven sharply serrated, oblong leaflets, hairy, blue-green.

Sepals red-brown longer than the purple petals. Fruits like small strawberries.

In boggy places. June and July. 3 feet.

(Comarum palustre L.)

(x) *(Lythraceae)*

37. Purple Loosestrife—*Lythrum salicaria L.*

Stem erect, somewhat branched. Leaves mostly in whorls or opposite; lanceolate with heart-shaped base. Flowers purple-red in a long, strong inflorescence, the flowers arranged in whorls. 12 stamens (sometimes 8).

June to September. 4 feet.

Of the 12 stamens, there are 6 short and 6 long. The style is short, medium or long. When the style is short, there are 6 very long and 6 shorter stamens. When the style is medium, there are 6 long and 6 short stamens. When the style is long, the stamens are 6 medium and 6 very short. This arrangement is called tri-morphism (3 forms) and ensures cross-pollination.

38. Water Purslane—*Peplis portula L.*

Stem procumbent, branching, somewhat red. Leaves opposite, obovate, blunt. Small, pink flowers in the leaf-axils. On boggy moors. Locally common. June to September. 10 inches.

(xi) WILLOW-HERBS *(Onagraceae)*

39. Great Hairy Willow-herb or Codlins and Cream— *Epilobium hirsutum L.*

Stem erect, with long, spreading hairs. Leaves in pairs, sessile, lanceolate with curved teeth. Flowers purple-red, ¾ inch across.

June to October. 5 feet.

Small-flowered Hairy Willow-herb— *Epilobium parviflorum Schr.*

Stem erect, with dense, soft hairs. Leaves lanceolate, distant teeth. Flowers about ⅜ inch across, light purple. four distinct stigma lobes.

July to August. 2 feet.

39a. **Rosebay or Fireweed**—*Chamaenerion angustifolium Scop.*

Stem erect, with strong, elongated inflorescence. Leaves spreading with conspicuous fine veins, lanceolate. Flowers with spreading, light purple petals. On moist ground. Commonest in the south. June to September. 5 feet.
(Epilobium angustifolium L.)

40. **Marsh Willow-herb**—*Epilobium palustre L.*

Stem erect, often with two rows of hairs. Leaves lanceolate, small, edges entire, mostly sessile. Flowers ⅜ inch across, rose-red. Stigma lobes permanent, bud-shaped. Flower-buds hanging.
Locally common. July and August. 2 feet.

Square-stemmed Willow-herb—*Epilobium obscurum Schreb.*

Stem has soft hairs above, with two or more somewhat raised lines. Leaves sparsely toothed, long, lanceolate, short hairs round the margin. Flowers ⅜ inch, pink.
Locally common. July and August. 3 feet.

41. **Marsh Ludwigia**—*Ludwigia palustris Ell.*

Small stems, sometimes growing in the mud, having at least some small roots. Leaves crosswise, pointed. Small green flowers in the leaf-axils.
In acid water, very local. July and August. 1 foot.

(xii) **MILFOILS** *(Haloragaceae)*

42. **Whorled Water Milfoil**—*Myriophyllum verticillatum L.*

Stem erect. Flowers held stiffly above the water. Leaves strongly divided in whorls of five or six. Flowers also in whorls, pink.
Not common. June to August. 1 foot.

PLATE IV

31. Hornwort; 31a. Prickly Hornwort; 32. Great Yellow Cress; 33. Common Water Cress;
34. Waterwort; 35. Meadow Sweet; 36. Marsh Cinquefoil; 37. Purple Loosestrife;
38. Water Purslane; 39. Great Hairy Willow-herb; 39a. Rosebay Willow-herb;
40. Marsh Willow-herb.

43. Spiked Water Milfoil—*Myriophyllum spicatum* L.
Stem erect like no. 42. Leaves strongly divided, except those between the flowers, in whorls of four. Flowers in whorls on spikes, pink.
In calcareous water. Locally common. July to September. 5 feet.

Alternate-flowered Water Milfoil—*Myriophyllum alterniflorum D.C.*
Stem erect, but above the water it bends when the flowers are closed. Leaves like no. 43. The pistillate flowers alternate with staminate ones on a short spike, and are yellow.
Locally common, especially in peaty water. May to August. 1 foot.

(xiii) *(Hippuridaceae)*

44. Mare's-tail—*Hippuris vulgaris* L.
Stem erect, tubular, held well out of water. Long, quick growing, branched rootstock. Leaves linear, in whorls of 8-12. Flowers in the leaf-axils, green.
Local. May to August. 3 feet.

(xiv) *(Hydrocotylaceae)*

45. Marsh Pennywort—*Hydrocotyle vulgaris* L.
Stem creeping. Leaves long-stalked, circular. Flowers reddish, in five to ten-flowered clusters.
In wet places, usually on acid soils. July to September. 10 inches.

(xv) *(Umbelliferae)*

46. Floating Marsh-wort—*Apium inundatum Rchb.*
Stem creeping in the mud or floating in the water. Submerged leaves bi-pinnate with linear leaflets. The upper leaves have broader leaflets, also pinnate. Flowers white, in two or three-rayed umbels.
June to August. 2 feet.

Creeping Cress—*Apium repens Lag.*
Stem creeping, leaves pinnate, leaflets rounder. Flowers white in three to six -rayed umbels.
In the water. Very rare. July to August. 1 foot.

Fool's Water Cress—*Apium nodiflorum Lag.*
Stem creeping, the last portion ascending. Leaves pinnate, ovate to lanceolate. Flowers greenish-white in six or more rayed umbels, with short peduncles.
Near the water. Common. June to September. 40 inches.

47. **Water Hemlock or Cowbane**—*Cicuta virosa L.*
Stem erect, as is also the rootstock, which has a series of air spaces inside. Leaves tri-pinnate with sharply serrated leaflets. Flowers white, in umbels without bracts, but many bracteoles. Grows on the bank. Very poisonous.
Rather rare. June to August. 4 feet.

48. **Water Parsnip**—*Sium latifolium L.*
Stem erect, angular and grooved. Leaves pinnate with sharply serrate leaflets. Submerged leaves with linear leaflets, bi-pinnate. Flowers white in terminal umbels. Poisonous.
Rather rare. July to August. 4 feet.

Narrow-leaved Water Parsnip—*Berula erecta Cov.*
Stem round, grooved. Leaves pinnate with oblong, serrate leaflets; the lower leaves rounder. Flowers white in short stalked umbels. Poisonous.
July to August. 2 feet.
(Sium erectum Huds.)

49. **Fine-leaved Water Dropwort**—*Oenanthe aquatica Poir.*
Strong, branched and grooved stem. Upper leaves bi-pinnate, submerged leaves at least tri-pinnate with small segments. Flowers white in six- to fourteen-rayed umbels without bracts.
June to August. 4 feet.

PLATE V

41. Marsh Ludwigia; 42. Whorled Water Milfoil; 43. Spiked Water Milfoil; 44. Mare's-tail;
45. Marsh Pennywort; 46. Floating Marsh-wort; 47. Water Hemlock; 48. Water Parsnip;
49. Fineleaved Water Dropwort; 50. Water Dropwort.

Parsley Water Dropwort—*Oenanthe lachenalii C.C. Gmel.*
Stem lined. Upper leaves pinnate, the lower leaves bi-pinnate. Flowers white in umbels with bracts.
July to September. 2 feet.

50. **Water Dropwort**—*Oenanthe fistulosa L.*
Stem hollow, as are also the petioles. Upper leaves single, lower leaves double pinnate, poorly developed. Flowers white with a red tinge, in three to eight-rayed, short stalked umbels. Petals unequal.
June to August. 2 feet.

51. **Wild Angelica**—*Angelica sylvestris L.*
Stem branched, round, lined and hollow. Leaves usually tri-pinnate with large, inflated sheaths. Flowers mostly white in many-rayed umbels.
July to September. 6 feet.

(xvi) *(Primulaceae)*

52. **Water Violet**—*Hottonia palustris L.*
Stem erect with submerged, deeply cut, comb-like leaves. Flowers mauve and yellow, five fused petals.
Mostly found in Eastern Counties. May to June. 18 inches.

53. **Tufted Loosestrife**—*Naumburgia thyrsiflora D.C.*
Stem erect. Leaves opposite, lanceolate, sessile, covered with black spots. Flowers golden-yellow, ⅓ inch diameter in long-stalked, dense clusters in the leaf-axils.
Rare. May to July. 2 feet.
(Lysimachia thyrsiflora L.)

Yellow Loosestrife—*Lysimachia vulgaris L.*
An erect stem with soft hairs, bearing short-stalked leaves, which are mostly in whorls. The flowers are larger, golden-yellow and arranged in a terminal inflorescence.
Locally common. June and July. 4 feet.

PLATE VI

51. Wild Angelica; 52. Water Violet; 53. Tufted Loosestrife; 54. Brookweed; 55. Larger Bindweed; 56. Bittersweet or Woody Nightshade; 57. Comfrey; 58. Figwort; 59. Mudwort.

54. Brookweed—*Samolus valerandi L.*

Erect, branched stem with radical leaves in a rosette and also spreading leaves which are entire. Flowers white with yellow centres in loose racemes. Mostly in brackish water. Locally common. July to September. 18 inches.

55. Larger Bindweed—*Calystegia sepium R. Br.*

Stem climbing, with heart-shaped, pointed leaves. Flowers white, sometimes pink.

Mainly in hedges or among reeds. June to September. 3 feet. *(Convolvulus sepium L.)*

56. Bittersweet or Woody Nightshade—*Solanum dulcamara L.*

Shrubby plant with long, twining, green stems. Leaves ovate, pointed, with small segments at the base. Flowers purple with green flecks surrounded by a white edge. June to August. 6 feet.

57. Comfrey—*Symphytum officinale L.*

Stem branched with oblong, decurrent leaves having rough, hairy surfaces and thick veins. Flowers purple, red or white, in double cymes.

Common, especially in the south. May to August. 3 feet.

58. Figwort—*Scrophularia nodosa L.*

Distinct four-angled stem, with opposite leaves, not hairy. Flowers greenish-yellow or brownish, in terminal panicle. June to September. 4 feet.

Water Figwort or Water Betony—*Scrophularia aquatica L.*
Distinct four-winged stem, petioles also winged.
June to September. 4 feet.
There are some sub-species of *Scrophularia aquatica.*

59. **Mudwort**—*Limosella aquatica* L.

Creeping rootstock with rosettes of oblong, long-stalked leaves. Small flowers, white or reddish; always closed when in the water. Grows on the banks or where water had flooded.

June to October. 2 inches.

60. **Brooklime**—*Veronica beccabunga* L.

The stem is cylindrical and hollow. The short-stalked, oval leaves are obtuse and arranged in pairs. The small, bright blue flowers are in racemes in the leaf-axils.

Common water or bank plant. May to September. 2 feet.

Water Speedwell—*Veronica anagallis-aquatica* L.
The stem is four-angled and hollow; sessile, oblong leaves, with pointed tips, are arranged in pairs. Small, light blue flowers, with darker lines, in racemes in the leaf-axils.
Water or bank plant. May to September. 2 feet.

61. **Red Rattle**—*Pedicularis palustris* L.

Erect, branched stem with spreading, deep-cut leaves. Flowers purplish-pink, forming two lips.
May to July. 1 foot.

(xxi) *(Lentibulariaceae)*

62. **Bladderwort**—*Utricularia vulgaris* L.

Submerged, thin, thread-like stems without roots. Leaves divided into fine segments bearing many small bladders. Small creatures are caught in these bladders and later digested. Flowers yellow, in clusters on long stems held above the water.

June to September. 1 foot.
There are three other species found in Great Britain.

63. **Water Mint**—*Mentha aquatica L.*

Square stem with side branches all ending in ball-shaped clusters of flowers. Similar flower clusters are also in the leaf-axils. Leaves oblong-ovate, short-stalked. Flowers lilac. Calyx with long teeth and dense hairs. Water plant but also found on banks.

June to September. 3 feet.

64. **Shore Weed**—*Littorella uniflora Asch.*

Leaves long and small in a radical rosette, on a creeping rootstock. There is a long-stemmed flower with stamens and also some short-stemmed flowers with single pistils. Flowers whitish.

Water or bank plants. Commoner in north.

June to August. 4 inches.

65. **Fringed Water Lily**—*Nymphoides peltata O.K.*

The stem creeps on the bottom with the tip growing upwards. The floating leaves are three-veined, almost round with deeply-cut, heart-shaped bases and long petioles. Large flowers, yellow, only held above the water when flowering. (See also no. 80).

Only in clear water. Local. July to September. 5 feet.

66. **Buckbean**—*Menyanthes trifoliata L.*

Thick, creeping rootstock with a very short, thick stem, having long-stalked, ternate leaves; the three leaflets fitting closely together. Flowers white, in long-stemmed panicles. Flower buds rose-red.

May to July. 1 foot.

PLATE VII

60. Brooklime; 61. Red Rattle; 62. Bladderwort; 63. Water Mint; 64. Shore Weed; 65. Fringed Water Lily; 66. Buckbean; 67. Marsh Bedstraw; 68. Valerian; 69. Water Lobelia.

67. Marsh Bedstraw—*Galium palustre L.*

Stem square, with four or five oblong leaves at each node. Leaves have a blunt tip and narrow base, only one vein. Flowers white. Anthers red.
May to September. 2 feet.

(xxvi) *(Valerianaceae)*

68. Valerian—*Valeriana officinalis L.*

The unbranched stem bears paired, pinnate leaves. Flowers pale pink, in thick, cushion-like clusters.
June to September. 3 feet.

(xxvii) *(Lobeliaceae)*

69. Water Lobelia—*Lobelia dortmanna L.*

Stem long and hollow, having flowers but practically no leaves. The leaves are radical, forming a rosette under the water; they are hollow and about 1½ inches long. Flowers white with blue corolla tubes.
Locally common in acid water. July to August. 2¼ feet.

(xxviii) *(Compositae)*

70. Hemp Agrimony—*Eupatorium cannabinum L.*

The erect stem has opposite, three-lobed leaves. Flowers purple, pink or white; growing in flat, cushion-like corymbs.
Grows on the bank. July to September. 5 feet.

71. Marsh Ragwort—*Senecio aquaticus Hill*

Erect stem with lobed or divided leaves. The lowest remain longer during fructification and are broader than the upper ones. Flowers: composite inflorescences with yellow ray-florets, together making a cushion-shaped corymb.
In marshy places. July to August. 2 feet.

Great Fen Ragwort—*Senecio paludosus L.*
The erect stem has undivided, toothed, sessile (or only short-stalked) leaves; which are felty underneath. The ray-florets are golden-yellow making a loose corymb.
Formerly native in Fen ditches, now appears to be extinct. June to August. 6 feet.

72. **Marsh Thistle**—*Cirsium palustre Scop.*
Prickly plant. Long, sparsely branched, erect stem, with long, narrow, undulately indented leaves. Flower-heads small, packed thickly together. Fruit-pappus feathery.
June to September. 5 feet.

Cirsium oleraceum Scop.
Erect stem with stem-clasping leaves; the lowest are deeply indented. Flower heads[1] large, surrounded by pale-coloured bracts. Petals pale-yellow.
Introduced; established locally in England and Scotland in marshy places. July to September. 2—5 feet.

73. **Marsh Sow Thistle**—*Sonchus palustris L.*
Erect, unbranched stem with narrow, sessile leaves. The leaves clasp the stem with the arrow-shaped base. They have fine teeth. Florets yellow, in heads, which together form a cushion-shaped mass.
Rare and decreasing. July to September. 10 feet.

(xxix) **WATER PLANTAINS** *(Alismataceae)*

74. **Arrowhead**—*Sagittaria sagittifolia L.*
A water plant. It is easily recognised by the arrow-shaped leaves held above the water on the triangular stems. The submerged leaves are not usually arrow-shaped. Flowers

---

[1] A flower system consisting of many florets attached to the enlarged top of the inflorescence axis, is called a "flower head" or capitulum. Usually this is surrounded by an involucre of bracts arranged in whorls.

PLATE VIII

70. Hemp Agrimony; 71. Marsh Ragwort; 72. Marsh Thistle; 73. Marsh Sow Thistle;
74. Arrowhead; 75. Common Water Plantain; 76. Floating Water Plantain; 77. Flowering
Rush; 78. Canadian Pondweed; 79. Water Soldier.

white, usually in whorls of three, the upper ones having only stamens, the lower ones having only a pistil.
Local, rarer in the north. June to August. 3 feet.

75. Common Water Plantain—*Alisma plantago-aquatica L.*

Upright stem with spoon-shaped, pointed leaves held above the water. The floating leaves are usually smaller. Flowers white or sometimes reddish, in a large ascending panicle, built up of whorls of flowers.
June to October. 5 feet.

Small-leaved Water Plantain—*Alisma gramineum Gmel.*
Like no. 75 but the leaves are much smaller. The submerged ones are mostly linear. Fruits with two grooves on the upper side.
Probably introduced. June to October. 4 feet.

Lesser Water Plantain—*Baldellia ranunculoides Parl.*
Erect stem with lanceolate leaves. Flowers white or sometimes red tinted, in a cushion-shaped whorl. Sometimes there are several whorls.
Locally common. May to August. 16 inches.
(*Echinodorus ranunculoides Engelm.*)

76. Floating Water Plantain—*Luronium natans Rafn.*

The floating stem bears long-stalked, lanceolate leaves above the water and linear, radical leaves below the water. Flowers white, five or less together at the nodes.
In mountain lakes, local. May to August. 3 feet.
(*Elisma natans Buch.*)

(xxx) *(Butomaceae)*

77. Flowering Rush—*Butomus umbellatus L.*

Stem erect, round. From the base arises a rosette of sturdy, erect leaves which are triangular in section. Flowers brown-red or whitish, in a cushion-like umbel at the top of the stem. Only three sepals and petals.

Local. June to August. 5 feet.

78. Canadian Pondweed—*Elodea canadensis Michx.*

The long, floating stem has small, oblong, finely-serrated leaves in whorls of three. Flowers white or purplish on slender stems above the water.

Introduced. Naturalised throughout Great Britain. Male plants very rare. May to August. 10 feet.

79. Water Soldier—*Stratiotes aloides L.*

Rosettes of spinous-serrate, long, stiff, grooved leaves. Flowers white, staminate flowers long-stalked; pistillate flowers shorter stalked and often enclosed in spiny bracts, resembling the claws of a crab.

In calcareous districts. Local, mainly in the Fens.

May to August. 1½ feet.

80. Frogbit—*Hydrocharis morsus-ranae L.*

Small stem with long roots; rosettes of long-stalked floating leaves and, in the autumn, runners with winter-buds. Leaves circular-cordate; at the base of the petiole are two transparent stipules. (Notice the difference from the Fringed Water Lily, no. 65.) Flower white: one large staminate or one small pistillate flower.

Usually in calcareous districts. Locally common.

June to August. 1 foot.

81. Opposite-leaved Pondweed—*Potamogeton densus L.*

Submerged plant with opposite, sessile, ovate leaves. Flowers green, above the water, in a sparsely-flowered spike.

Locally abundant. June to October. 1½ feet.

82. **Fennel-leaved Pondweed**—*Potamogeton pectinatus L.*

The slender, strongly branched stem has spreading, linear leaves, with distinct lateral veins and a stipular sheath about 2 inches long. Flowers in groups on a long stem held above the water forming a loose spike.

Common. June to August. 10 feet.

83. **Fen Pondweed**—*Potamogeton coloratus Horn.*

The slender, branched stem has spreading, transparent, stalked leaves. The petiole is half as long as the leaf-blade which is ovate and rather pointed in the floating form and lanceolate in the submerged leaves.

In Fens. Local. June to September. 2 feet.

84. **Grass-wrack Pondweed**—*Potamogeton compressus L.*

The somewhat winged stem has grass-shaped leaves with an obtuse tip bearing a small spine. More than ten flowers in a long-stalked spike.

Local. July to August. 5 feet.

Sharp-leaved Pondweed—*Potamogeton acutifolius Link.*
The somewhat winged stem has grass-shaped leaves with a more gradually pointed tip. Six (or less) flowers in a short-stalked spike between much longer leaves.

Rare. 2 feet.

Grassy Pondweed—*Potamogeton obtusifolius M. and K.*
The somewhat compressed stem has grass-shaped leaves with a blunt top and a small point. Short, six to eight-flowered spike, with a stalk of about the same length as the spike itself.

Local. June to August. 3 feet.

Flat-stalked Pondweed—*Potamogeton friesii Rupr.*
The somewhat compressed stem has linear leaves with blunt or pointed tips, having distinct lateral veins. Short,

PLATE IX

80. Frogbit; 81. Opposite-leaved Pondweed; 82. Fennel-leaved Pondweed; 83. Fen Pondweed; 84. Grass-wrack Pondweed; 85. Hair-like Pondweed; 86. Curled Pondweed;
87. Perfoliate Pondweed; 88. Various-leaved Pondweed; 89. Broad-leaved Pondweed.

six to ten-flowered spikes, with a stalk three times as long as the spike itself.

Common on mud bottom. June to August. 4 feet.

(Potamogeton mucronatus Schrad.)

Slender Pondweed—*Potamogeton pusillus L.*

The round, strongly branched stem has linear leaves (not more than $\frac{1}{10}$ inch broad), with pointed tips, without lateral veins. Only two or three flowers in a long-stalked spike. Not uncommon, mostly in calcareous waters.

June to September. $1\frac{1}{2}$ feet.

85. **Hair-like Pondweed**—*Potamogeton trichoides Cham. and Schld.*

The round stem has hair-like leaves with only one vein. Long-stalked spike with four to eight flowers.

Chiefly in south and east England. June and July. 2 feet.

86. **Curled Pondweed**—*Potamogeton crispus L.*

The $\pm$ four-angled stem has sessile, lanceolate leaves with finely serrated and undulated margins and distinct net-veins. Common. May to September. 3 feet.

87. **Perfoliate Pondweed**—*Potamogeton perfoliatus L.*

The round stem has very broad leaves, which are so strongly stem-clasping that they seem to be perfoliate. Common. June to August. 3 feet.

Long-stalked Pondweed—*Potamogeton praelongus Wulf.*

The round stem is rather zig-zagged. The leaves are sessile, oblong-lanceolate and somewhat clasping. The leaf-tip is hooded. The spike stalk may become 8 inches long and is evenly thickened.

Local. June to August. 10 feet.

Reddish Pondweed—*Potamogeton alpinus Balb.*

The round stem has floating and submerged, often reddish, leaves. Floating leaves are stalked, ovate; the submerged

leaves are sessile and lanceolate. Many-flowered spike with a long, evenly thickened stalk.
Throughout Britain, but local and rare in south and east England. June to August. 2 feet.

88. **Various-leaved Pondweed**—*Potamogeton gramineus L.*
The round stem has submerged, pointed, grass-like leaves and, sometimes, long-stalked, ovate-elliptical, floating leaves. Long, many-flowered spikes with stalks which are stout, as long as the spike, and thickened upwards.
Locally common. Chiefly in acid water. June to August. 4 feet.

Shining Pondweed—*Potamogeton lucens L.*
Totally submerged plant, with short-stalked, shiny, lanceolate leaves, the edges being wavy or toothed.
Locally common. In calcareous waters. June to August. 10 feet.

89. **Broad-leaved Pondweed**—*Potamogeton natans L.*
The unbranched stem has small, oval, floating leaves and, before the flowering time, channelled, small, submerged leaves. The leathery, floating leaves have a petiole channelled on the upper side. Thick, loose spike with a short stalk.
Common in shallow water. June to August. 5 feet.

Bog Pondweed—*Potamogeton polygonifolius Pourr.*
Unbranched stem. Floating leaves lanceolate, with broad but not grooved, petioles. Submerged leaves have long petioles, bluntly lanceolate. Short spike with a short stalk.
Common. Usually in acid water. June to August. 2 feet.
(Potamogeton oblongus Viv.)

(xxxiii) *(Ruppiaceae)*

90. **Sea Ruppia or Beaked Tassel Pondweed**—*Ruppia maritima L.*
Submerged plant with thread-like leaves which have broad

33

sheaths, about 4 inches long. Paired flowers on a short or long stalk. Flowers have two stamens and four pistils.
In brackish water. Local. June to August. 1½ feet.

91. **Horned Pondweed**—*Zannichellia palustris L.*

The long, thread-like and strongly branched stem bears long, thread-like leaves but without sheaths. (This last point distinguishes it from no. 82). Flowers apparently in the leaf-axils. There are staminate flowers with two stamens, or pistillate flowers with two pistils bearing funnel-shaped stigmas.
Completely submerged. In fresh or brackish water. Locally common. May to August. 1½ feet.

Zannichellia pedicellata Whlnbg.
(May be only a variety)
Can be distinguished from the previous one by the fruits which are on ± $\frac{1}{20}$ inch long stems; while those of no. 91 are on shorter stalks or, more usually, are sessile.
Locally common in brackish water.

92. **Holly-leaved or Greater Naiad**—*Najas marina L.*

The dichotomously branched stem bears opposite, lanceolate, serrated leaves having prickles on the underside and large smooth-edged sheaths. The stem is also prickly. Staminate flowers with one stamen or pistillate flowers with one pistil. Possibly only female flowers in Britain.
In brackish water. June to August. 20 inches.

Slender or Flexible Naiad—*Najas flexilis Ros. und Sch.*
Can be distinguished from the previous species because there are no prickles on the stem or the underside of the leaves and the leaf-edges are more finely toothed.
Local. June to August. 10 inches.

93. Jointed Rush—*Juncus articulatus L.*

A grass-like plant with long, thick, spiky leaves divided internally, by cross-partitions, into little compartments. The flower leaves are all of the same length with a spiky tip. Inflorescence: many clusters together on the tip of the stem. Fruit pointed. Abundant, especially on acid soils.

July and August. 2 feet.

Hard Rush—*Juncus inflexus L.*

In the strongly grooved stem, the pith is divided by cross-partitions. Leaves are sheathing, brown, shiny and radical, while the stem is a dull, sea-green. There is an erect bract which lengthens the stem and in the axil of which is a loose cluster of small flowers. Small fruits with pointed tips.

June to August. 2 feet.

Soft Rush—*Juncus effusus L.*

Smooth, bright green stem with divisions in the pith. Sheathing, radical leaves, a dull, light brown. Again there is an erect bract with a loose flower cluster. Flowers with three stamens. Fruits indented at the top.

June to August. 2 feet.

Blunt-flowered Rush—*Juncus subnodulosus Schr.*

The leaves are, like the stems, divided internally by cross-partitions. The flowers are in a loose cluster, the lateral axes of which are bent.

Locally abundant, especially on calcareous peat.

June and July. 4 feet.

94. Sea Club-rush—*Scirpus maritimus L.*

Triangular, rather rough stems, arising from a rootstock, which forms turnip-shaped thickenings. The lowest bract rises above the inflorescence. The small clusters are up to $\frac{3}{4}$ inch long.

Locally abundant on muddy banks near the sea.
June to October. 3½ feet.

95. **Bulrush**—*Schoenoplectus lacustris Pall.*
Plant with long stems ± ½ inch thick, arising from a sturdy rootstock. Under the branched flower stalks there is one bract which lengthens the stem. Each flower has three pistils.
July to August. 10 feet.

96. **Common Spike Rush**—*Eleocharis palustris R. and Sch.*
A creeping rootstock with radical leaves which are in single bracts, and a rolled, dull, darker green stem, bearing a single compact inflorescence on the top. The spike has many flowers. Each flower has two pistils. The lowest bract encloses half the inflorescence.
May to August. 2 feet.
(Scirpus palustris L.)

96a. **One-glumed Spike Rush**—*Eleocharis uniglumis Sch.*
Differs from the former in that the lowest bract encloses the whole inflorescence. The stem is lighter green and shiny.
May to August. 1 foot.

97. **Floating Mud Rush**—*Eleogiton fluitans Link.*
Large, often branched stem, floating loosely in the water and has linear leaves. At the top of the flower stalk is a single spike without any bracts.
Local. June and August. 1 foot.
(Scirpus fluitans L.)

98. **False Fox Sedge**—*Carex otrubae Podp.*
Plant turf-forming. Stem sharply three-angled, rough above, not hollow. At the base are light brown bracts. Spikes light brown. Fruits distinctly ribbed, smooth.
June. 3 feet.
(Carex nemorosa Rebent.)

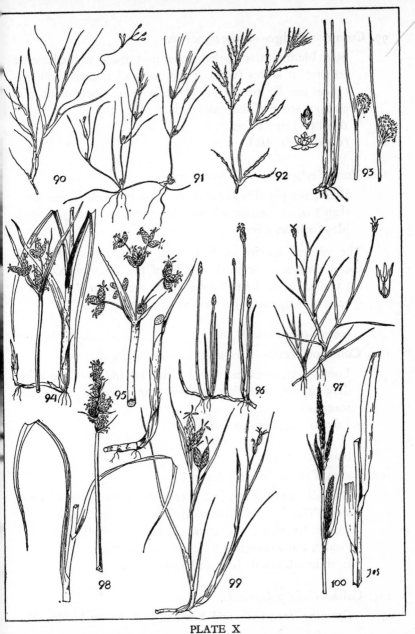

PLATE X

90. Sea Ruppia; 91. Horned Pondweed; 92. Holly-leaved Najas; 93. Jointed Rush; 94. Sea Club-rush; 95. Bulrush; 96. Common Spike Rush; 97. Floating Mud Rush; 98. False Fox Sedge; 99. Common Sedge; 100. Pond Sedge.

99. **Common Sedge**—*Carex nigra Rch.*

Stem bluntly three-angled, upper part rough, at the base are rosettes of leaves (without flowers) and runners. Inflorescences usually consist of two spikes with pistillate flowers and one spike of staminate flowers at the top.
April to June. 2 feet.
(Carex fusca All.)

100. **Pond Sedge**—*Carex riparia Curt.*

Erect, sharply three-angled, rough stem with leaves more than ⅔ of an inch broad; margins entire or, rarely, frayed.
May to June. 4 feet.

The various species of Sedge are difficult to identify. A useful characteristic is the shape of the bracts surrounding the fruits. In the British Isles there are about 80 different species of Sedge and they also form many hybrids.

(xxxviii) *(Gramineae)*

101. **Common Reed**—*Phragmites communis Trin.*

Long, erect, stout stems with rather broad leaves and large, dark brown, spreading panicles. Long, deeply penetrating rootstock.
July to October. 10 feet.

(xxxix) *(Araceae)*

102. **Sweet Flag**—*Acorus calamus L.*

A spadix apparently arises laterally from the flattened, erect stem. This is only "apparently" because the sheath of the spadix lengthens the stem. Leaves sword-shaped with, locally, wavy margins. A very thick rootstock.
Introduced. Local. June and July. 4 feet.

103. **Calla**—*Calla palustris L.*

Creeping rootstock and heart-shaped, entire leaves. The

flower spadix is club-shaped with a sheath, the outer side of which is green, the inner white. Fruit is a red berry. Introduced. Naturalised in wet woods in Surrey. May and June. 1 foot.

(xl) DUCKWEEDS *(Lemnaceae)*

104. **Great Duckweed**—*Spirodela polyrrhiza Schleiden*
All Duckweeds have flattened leaf-like stems which can be found floating in the water, on the surface or submerged. The flowers arise on what appears to be the leaf-margin. Each flower consists of a stamen and a pistil. In this species there are two or more rootlets on each plant; the underside is usually reddish.
Local. May to June. $\frac{1}{8}$ inch.
(Lemna polyrrhiza L.)

Ivy-leaved Duckweed—*Lemna trisulca L.*
Submerged plants with oblong, pointed, crowded thalli (leaf-like stems). Each thallus has one rootlet. Each thallus arises at an angle to the older one.
April to May. $\frac{2}{3}$ inch.

Lesser Duckweed—*Lemna minor L.*
Floating plant. The thalli are broad, flat and green. One rootlet on each.
April to June. $\frac{1}{8}$ inch.

Gibbous Duckweed—*Lemna gibba L.*
Floating plant. Thalli flat above, convex below. One rootlet.
April to June. Local. $\frac{1}{4}$ inch.

Rootless Duckweed—*Wolffia arrhiza Wimm.*
Floating plant, without roots. Thalli lens-shaped.
Rare. Seldom flowers. About $\frac{1}{20}$ inch.

(xli) BUR-REEDS *(Sparganiaceae)*

105. **Small Bur-reed**—*Sparganium minimum Wallr.*
Stem is floating, sometimes almost upright. The leaves are

as long as the stem, small, very thin and without a mid-rib. Inflorescences unbranched; there are two or three globose heads of pistillate flowers and one or two globose heads of staminate flowers.

June to August. 3 feet.

106. Branched Bur-reed—*Sparganium erectum L.*

Strong, erect stem with broad, upright, truncated leaves, triangular due to a sharp keel on the underside. Inflorescence usually branched, sometimes the lowest branches of it have heads of pistillate flowers and on the other branches are four or more heads bearing staminate flowers.

Bank or bog plant. June to September. 3 feet.

(*Sparganium ramosum Huds.*)

107. Floating Bur-reed—*Sparganium angustifolium Michx.*

The stem is floating, as are the leaves which are flat on the upper side, convex on the lower and which have a distinct mid-rib. The bracts subtending the inflorescences are stem-clasping and longer than the inflorescences.

June to August. Mainly in mountainous districts. 3 feet.

108. Unbranched Bur-reed—*Sparganium simplex Huds.*

The erect stem has leaves less than $\frac{2}{8}$ inch across; the leaf-bases are wide, above the leaf-base the blade is narrow, but it becomes broader towards the top. Inflorescence has one flower head with pistillate and four or more with staminate flowers.

June to July. 2 feet.

(xlii) REED MACES *(Typhaceae)*

109. Great Reed Mace—*Typha latifolia L.*

The erect stem has broad, linear leaves, arranged on the stem in two distinct rows. The long, erect spike is divided into two parts, the lower part has pistillate flowers (one pis-

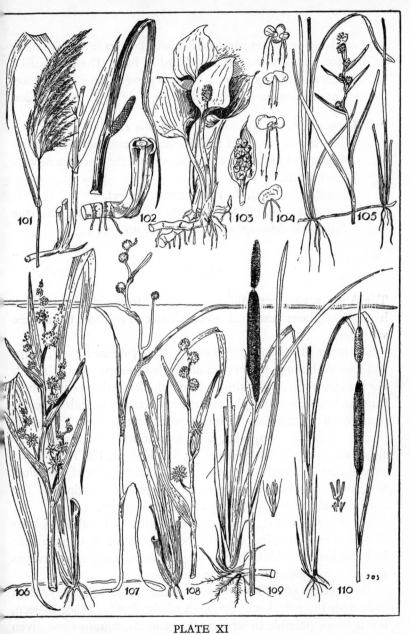

PLATE XI

101. Common Reed; 102. Sweet Flag; 103. Calla; 104. Great Duckweed; 105. Small
Bur-reed; 106. Branched Bur-reed; 107. Floating Bur-reed; 108. Unbranched Bur-reed;
109. Great Reed Mace; 110. Lesser Reed Mace.

til) and the upper part has staminate flowers (each with three stamens). The corolla is reduced to hairs. There is usually only a small gap between the two parts of the inflorescence. Common, especially in the south. July to August. 8 feet.

110. **Lesser Reed Mace**—*Typha angustifolia L.*
The leaves are small and linear. The two parts of the inflorescence are more widely separated, the pistillate flowers have bracts.
Locally common. July to August. 10 feet.
The plants are often incorrectly called Bulrushes. The true Bulrush is *Schoenoplectus lacustris* (see no. 95).

ALGAE

The Algae have a very different structure from the plants which have already been described, so it is better to consider them quite separately.

The other plants have more or less clearly defined roots, stems and leaves (although the mosses do not have proper roots). This is not the case in the Algae, although some look as if they possess these features. In the stem-like parts there are never any vascular bundles (the groups of fine tubes which transport water and sap). The whole plant-body is like a somewhat branched leaf, and for this reason the algae belong to the "leaf-plants" or Thallophyta. The Thallophyta vary a great deal both in structure and in their mode of reproduction, so it is impossible to give a brief general description. The Bacteria and Fungi also belong to the Thallophyta.

It is not possible to see much of the structure of the algae without using a microscope, but some of the microscopic algae have been included here, in addition to the larger species, because their names are often mentioned in books on water plants.

The green algae *(Chlorophyceae)* are the easiest to identify, often even with the naked eye, although all the details cannot be seen, but it is not possible to separate the main filamentous algae given together in no. 3 without using a microscope. They usually appear as a slimy, greenish mass.

Reproduction of the filamentous algae is usually by means of zoospores (3E). These come out of the cell-wall, form flagella and swim freely in the water; eventually they settle and grow into new threads. Alternatively certain plants may form male or female cells (3B and 3C), these 'gametes' fuse and later a new thread forms.

Spirogyra and *Zygnema* belong to the *Conjugales*, as they have another method of reproduction. Two threads lie together so that they touch, then small outgrowths arise from opposite cells and these grow together so that the cells are connected by a tube. The contents of the cells gradually come together so that they form a compact mass which can pass the winter as a thick-walled spore. In the spring each of these gives rise to a new thread.

In addition to these larger green algae, there are also a large number of unicellular algae, for example the species *Zoochorella vulgaris B.*, which lives inside small animals (usually hydras) and gives them their green colour.

There are no brown algae *(Phaeophyceae)* in the ponds or streams, but there are a few red ones *(Rhodophyceae)*. The blue-green algae *(Cyanophyceae)* are all very small, but sometimes they can be recognised by the colour they give to the water. *Microcystis aeruginosa* and species of *Oscillaria* (these small algae have no English names) will make the water look as if it contains green paint; while species of *Lyngbia* form a blue-green or black mass on rotten leaves in stagnant water. Some of the colony-forming blue-green algae are visible to the naked eye.

In the descriptions which follow some main details for identification have been given.

1. Stoneworts—*Chara sp.*

This alga has a jointed, central axis with root-like processes for attachment at the bottom. At the nodes are whorls of radiating branches and in the axes of these there may be new main axes. The alga thus looks like a water-plant with needle-shaped leaves. It is very brittle, owing to deposits of lime. The side branches also appear jointed and bear both male and female reproductive organs, the male being orange coloured (1a, 1b.). The female organ has a small crown on the top, made of five cells. Main axis —± 10 inches.

2. *Nitella sp.*

Rather like the previous one but smaller and without the calcareous deposits. The crown on the female organ is made of ten cells.

3. Filamentous Algae

A. *Tribonema sp.*

Long threads (0.008 ins. thick), at first attached but later free-floating. Large cells, with thick walls and large, green chloroplasts. The drawing also shows the formation of the reproductive cells (zoospores).

B. *Ulothrix sp.*

Branched filaments of cells, each cell with one large chloroplast. Reproduces by large and small motile gametes. These fuse in pairs and form a resting spore, which eventually grows into a new thread.

C. *Cladophora sp.*

Branched filaments forming a bushy mass, which may grow to ± 8 inches in length. May reproduce by forming a large spore with two flagella (b) but usually forms many small spores from a terminal cell (a).

D. *Chaetophora sp.*

Long, cylindrical, branched threads forming a bushy mass, the side branches bearing long, colourless hairs. The threads may form a gelatinous mass.

E. *Vaucheria sp.*

Long, thin, very branched threads, which are not divided into definite cells. Reproduces both asexually, by zoospores,

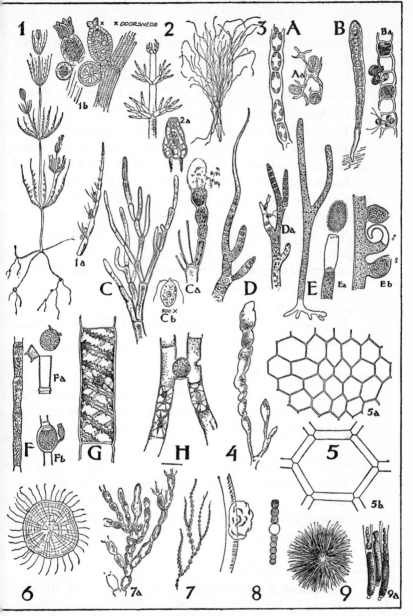

PLATE XII

1. Stonewort (shown in section at the right of fig. 1b, at X); 2. *Nitella*; 3. Filamentous Algae. A. *Tribonema*, B. *Ulothrix*, C. *Cladophora*, D. *Chaetophora*, E. *Vaucheria*, F. *Oedogonium*, G. *Spirogyra*, H. *Zygnaema*; 4. *Enteromorpha intestinalis*; 5. Water-net; 6. *Chaetopeltis orbicularis*; 7. Frog-spawn Alga; 8. Nostoc; 9. Hedgehog Weed.

formed at the tips of the threads (a) and also sexually, when both male and female sex organs are formed (b). The plant forms thick green clusters on the sides of ornamental ponds etc. and is often the green "weed" at the bottom of a stream.

F. *Oedogonium sp.*

Long, unbranched threads. Reproduces asexually by zoospores. In sexual reproduction a small zoospore is formed; this attaches itself to the side of a cell in which an egg-cell has been formed. The zoospore gives rise to two spermatozoids, one of which combines with the egg-cell.

G. *Spirogyra sp.*

The long threads are made of longish, cylindrical cells. Each cell has one or more spiral chloroplasts and one nucleus. *Spirogyra* is found on stones and water-plants in still water forming a green, slimy mass.

H. *Zygnaema sp.*

Like *Spirogyra* but has two star-shaped chloroplasts in each cell.

4. *Enteromorpha intestinalis Link.*

Membranous, hollow, swollen tubes. Yellow-green. Fixed when young but later drift about freely. May reach 40 inches in length and be 1 inch wide.

5. **Water-net**—*Hydrodictyon reticulatum Lagerh.*

Loose, floating colonies of cylindrical cells, which are attached at the corners, so that the whole colony forms a network, with six-sided spaces. The whole colony can become quite large. (5a— natural size. 5b— enlarged.)

6. *Chaetopeltis orbicularis B.*

The thallus is made of cells which form a round, flat disc, fringed by long hairs. Occurs mostly on the undersides of water plants. Disc about $\frac{1}{25}$ inch diameter.

7. **Frog-spawn Alga**—*Batrachospermum monoliforme Roth.*

This is a red alga, having the chlorophyll in the thallus hidden by a red pigment (phycoerythrin), so that the effect is of a violet or brown-green colour. It is in the form of long, branched threads; the beaded effect is due to a series of gelatinous masses. Reproduces sexually. 8 inches. (7a— enlarged).

8. **Nostoc**—*Nostoc parmelioides Kütz.*

This is a blue-green alga, forming thread-like colonies of spherical cells. It forms a slimy, brown-green mass which is spherical or barrel-shaped (2 inches), and is attached to underwater objects.

9. **Hedgehog Weed**—*Rivularia echinulata P. Richter*

Also a blue-green colonial alga. Each plant consists of a single cell but the cells are enclosed in a mucous layer to form thread-like colonies ($\frac{1}{16}$ inch) and these adhere together to form a spherical mass. It contains chlorophyll and also a bluish pigment (phycocyanin). On the underside of each thread is a large cell which does not divide (heterocyst).

ANIMALS

When any particular pond or stream is studied, one can be sure to find many animals living there, particularly among the clumps of plants. Many of them are very small and difficult to discover with the naked eye. There are many species which one can only see by using a high-powered microscope. These are the plankton animals. To obtain them it is necessary to use a net of fine gauze.

It is not possible to identify all the animals at once just by using the illustrations; in many cases it is useful to study them under a microscope, when a complete identification may be made.

For this purpose it is most convenient if the animals are bred in an aquarium so that they can be studied quietly. In this way one can soon identify many species and also observe details of their mode of life.

In these kinds of observations amateurs have often made interesting discoveries which the scientists have missed.

In this book none of the very small animals have been drawn, except for those which form colonies or are normally found in large groups so that they can be easily seen.

In many animals the males can be distinguished from the females by differences in body structure, size, colour etc. In the pictures and the descriptions this has been indicated by using the common symbols for male and female. ♂ means male; ♀ means female. It is impossible to get them wrong if one remembers that the male symbol represents a shield and a spear, and the female symbol represents a hand-mirror.

SPONGES *(Porifera)*

Sponges are often found in fresh water fixed firmly to plants and to submerged objects. They can be seen to form encrustations on stones and also branching masses, so that it is impossible to identify them from their shape.

All freshwater sponges are the encrusting type; when they are pulled out of water there is a most disagreeable smell, so that one tends not to look at them too closely. On examination they can be seen to contain many branching canals. From these run many smaller canals and there is a large, central space. The sponges are mostly colonial and one can find more than one central hole in a colony.

The body is made up of many different cells; for example, flagellated cells, which are found in definite bladder-shaped spaces in the body wall and are responsible for setting up a water current. The water is drawn in through the small openings of the canal system, collects in the centre and leaves the body through the large central hole or osculum.

The sponges feed on small organisms which are in the water and are carried in with the water current. Special cells are responsible for digestion and others for the formation of a skeleton. In the freshwater sponges this is a soft, elastic mass made of spongin (a horny material), which may, however, have siliceous needles (spicules) embedded in it.

The so-called sponge of daily life is a spongin-skeleton from an animal which lives in the Mediterranean Sea. This skeleton clearly shows the canal system of the animal (spicules are not found in it).

The freshwater sponges reproduce by means of eggs; these hatch as larvae, which have a short, free-swimming existence before attaching themselves and growing into a new sponge. To pass the winter these sponges form gemmules. These are small balls, consisting of a group of cells, with a protective covering. The covering has a small opening and often contains prettily-shaped spicules, having at each end a shield-shaped disc (called amphidiscs). The presence or absence of these amphidiscs and their shape are useful points for identification but one needs a good microscope to examine them properly. For the sake of completeness a few of the freshwater sponges are mentioned here with details of the gemmules.

1. **Pond Sponge**—*Euspongilla lacustris (L.)*

In stagnant water it takes on a branched appearance but in running water it forms an encrustation (fig. 1a). Usually grass-green in colour but in shaded places and in running water it is yellowish. The gemmules have no amphidiscs, the opening is not tubular (fig. 1b). Common in ponds.

2. *Spongilla fragilis Leidy.*

Less common. Forms a thin yellow or grey crust on stones etc. Gemmules have no amphidiscs, but the opening is definitely tubular. The skeleton is poorly developed, as is the whole sponge (fig. 2).

3. *Trochospongilla erinaceus Ehrbg.*

Encrusting. Amphidiscs smooth (fig. 3).

4. **River Sponge**—*Ephydatia fluviatilis (L.).*

Encrusting with small projections. Common under stones in rivers and canals. Amphidiscs with long axes and star-shaped end-plates (fig. 4a).

5. *Ephydatia mulleri (Liebk.)*

Also encrusting with small projections. The amphidiscs have star-shaped end-plates but short axes (fig. 5).

COELENTERATES *(Coelenterata)*

The coelenterates are all very simply formed animals and no highly developed structures or sense organs can be seen. Like the sponges, they are characterised by having a central space but there are no fine canals for the water to enter, as in the sponges. There is only one opening which has to serve as both a mouth and an anus.

The body of the coelenterates is made up of two layers of cells between which is a structureless supporting layer. The outer layer contains stinging cells, each containing a small vesicle in which is a coiled, hollow thread. When a projection of the cell is touched, the thread is shot out and pierces the prey. At the same time poison is poured out which will paralyse the prey. The larger, marine coelenterates, like the jellyfish, can be dangerous to man if the poison actually enters the blood. The freshwater coelenterates are small and the stings would not be strong enough to penetrate the human skin. As well as being wounded by the stings, the prey remains fixed by them to the tentacles, so that it cannot escape.

There are three classes of coelenterates, namely the hydroids

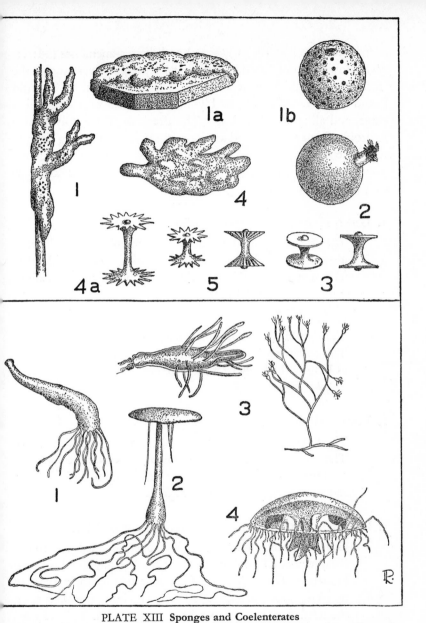

PLATE XIII **Sponges and Coelenterates**

SPONGES: 1. Pond Sponge, branching and encrusting colonies and gemmules; 2. Gemmule of *Spongilla fragilis*; 3. Amphidisc of *Trochospongilla erinaceus*; 4. River Sponge, encrusting colony and amphidisc; 5. Amphidisc of *Ephydatia mulleri*.

COELENTERATES: 1. Green Hydra; 2. Brown Hydra on Duckweed; 3. Brackish Water Polyp, a polyp and a colony; 4. Fresh Water Jellyfish

(Hydrozoa), the jellyfish *(Scyphozoa)* and the sea-anemones *(Antho-zoa)*. However, only the hydroids have representatives among the fresh and brackish water forms. The main type of hydroid found in fresh water is the Hydra, which has only the polyp stage, and all species are single. The Brackish Water Polyps, also hydroids, form colonies and are more specialised in having definite reproductive individuals. The gonophores, as the reproductive polyps are called, can easily be seen in the branched colonies as they have no tentacles.

1. **Green Hydra**—*Chlorohydra viridissima (Pall.)*

The green colour, caused by the presence of small green algae in the body wall, makes this species easy to identify. The tentacles are shorter than the body, which is about ¼ inch long. Found in still water.
(Hydra viridis L.)

Slender Hydra—*Hydra vulgaris attenuata*
The colour varies; it is sometimes orange. The tentacles are as long as the body or a little longer.
(Hydra attenuata)

2. **Brown Hydra**—*Pelmatohydra oligactis (Pall.)*

The lower part of the body is narrowed to a distinct stalk. The colour varies: grey, brown or reddish. The tentacles are longer than the body, which may be up to an inch long. In slow-moving water. *(Hydra fusca L.)*

3. **Brackish Water Polyp**—*Cordylophora lacustris Allm.*

Colonial form, with a root-like portion fixed to stones. Rosy-white. The colony is about 2 inches high and is much branched. The ordinary polyps have usually more than 20 tentacles which are scattered over the body (see fig. 3 on the left). The gonophores have no tentacles. The colonies often become detached and form tangled masses which get caught in fishing nets. In winter the black root-like portion remains, with short, dark 'branches' into which the softer parts are withdrawn.

Found in some estuaries and on the Norfolk Broads.

(Cordylophora caspia var. lacustris Allm.)

4. **Fresh Water Jellyfish**—*Craspedacusta marginata (Modeer)*

The full-sized animal may be ¾ inch across, but it is usually undeveloped. It remains small in cool water ($\frac{1}{10}$ inch). The jellyfish has a mouth tube with 4 short 'arms'; there are many (200-400) tentacles and on the edge of the umbrella is a 'shelf' or velum with balance organs (statocysts). The polyp form is very small and inconspicuous.

Very rare. *(Craspedacusta sowerbii Lank.)*

WORMS *(Vermes)*[1]

The Worms embrace a wide variety of forms. As it is not possible to include them all, only the commoner examples are given. There has been no attempt to classify the different kinds of worm.

Most worms (except the Bryozoa, which are considered separately) are elongated animals moving by means of well-developed muscles, which are alternately stretched and contracted. The ordinary worms have also stiff bristles which prevent them from slipping back. Some worms have suckers which help them to move as well as to attach themselves.

Most worms have great powers of regeneration, especially the flatworms (nos. 1, 2 and 3).

The different species may or may not show segmentation; the number an arrangement of the eyes will vary, the presence or absence of bristles can be noted. All these points are useful for identification.

---

[1] We are undebted to Mr A. J. D. Veen for his expert advice on this section of the book.

A. FLATWORMS *(Platyhelminthes)*

1. **Brown Flatworm**—*Dugesia lugubris (O.C.Sch.)*
   Soft, flat worm. Yellow-brown to black. The head is slightly rounded and has two eyes surrounded by white areas. ± ¾ inch. Eggs in spherical egg-sacs attached to water-plants by small stalks. In stagnant water.
   Dugesia gonocephala—similar, but the head is more triangular.

2. **Black Flatworm**—*Polycelis nigra Ehrbg.*
   Head bluntly triangular with many eyes along the edge of the body. Black. ⅔ inch. Common.
   Polycelis tenuis Ijima—similar, but more brown or grey.

3. **White Flatworm**—*Dendrocoelum lacteum (O.F.M.)*
   Milky-white flatworm. Head slightly three-lobed with movable lobes; the front edge is practically straight. The branched digestive system is clearly visible. Two eyes. 1¼ inches.

B. HAIRWORMS *(Nematomorpha)*

4. **Hairworm**—*Gordius aquaticus L.*
   Long, thin, cylindrical worm. Generally dark brown, the front part is lighter and has a darker ring. The ♀ is lighter. The abdomen of the ♀ is cylindrical, that of the ♂ forked. No mouth or anus. The ♂ s and ♀ s are found entwined together in masses with the eggs, laid in strings, between the bodies. ± 10 inches or longer.
   The larva is parasitic on insects.

C. ROUND WORMS *(Nematoda)*

5. *Dorylamius stagnalis Duj.*
   A small, thin, thread-like worm, less than ⅔ inch long. The head is sharply pointed (fig. 5b), forming a sharp spine. Lives among the roots of plants or among the Bryozoa etc.

D. SEGMENTED WORMS *(Annelida)*

6. **Iridescent Nereis**—*Nereis diversicolor Müll.*

    Body divided into many (90-120) segments, which project into stumpy structures (parapodia) bearing tiny bristles (see fig. 6b). Dark flesh colour with a dark-red, longitudinal line down the back due to the underlying blood-vessel. Iridescent. $\pm$ 6 inches.

    Occasionally migrates into brackish water from estuaries.

7. *Chaetogaster diaphanus Gruith.*

    About $\frac{2}{3}$ inch long. A cylindrical worm with two rows of bristles, arranged in groups.

    Chaetogaster limnaei B.
    Parasitic on snails. About $\frac{1}{10}$ inch long.

8. *Stylaria lacustris L.*

    About $\frac{2}{3}$ inch long. A cylindrical, transparent worm with two rows of long bristles, usually in pairs. The head projects in a long proboscis and has two eyes. Found wriggling among water-plants, especially among the rootlets of duckweed.

    Reproduction can take place by transverse division so that two animals are formed from one. Under the microscope, contractions of the gut can be seen.

    (Nais lacustris L.) (Nais proboscidea Müll.)

    Nais elinguis O.F.M.
    Can be distinguished from the previous one by the absence of the proboscis and the much shorter bristles. Each can divide into two animals. It swims well. $\frac{3}{4}$ inch.

9. **Tube Worm**—*Tubifex rivilorum Lam.*

    About $1\frac{3}{4}$ inches long. These worms live in the mud from which they make tubes into which they can withdraw. They are found in places where there is suitable food, eg. the

drainage from a food factory. The worms wriggle about in
the water. They are red coloured, owing to the blood which
is visible through the skin. They are often used as food for
fish kept in aquaria.

10. **White Pot Worm**— *Enchytraeus albidus Henle*

Small, white worm with four rows of bristles. Lives in mud,
clustered among plants growing on stones, etc. Common.
⅔ inch.

11. **Brittle Pot Worm**—*Lumbriculus variegatus (O.F.M.)*

Up to 4 inches long, a greenish, iridescent worm with
two rows of bristles. The gut, when filled, is visible through
the skin as a series of black spots. Great powers of regeneration. The animal breaks at a slight touch and each part can
grow into a new, fully-formed worm.

12. **Fish Leech**—*Piscicola geometra (L.)*

A small (1-2 inches), round, blood-sucker with a small
sucker round the mouth and a large one on the abdomen.
On the back are green markings with a white stripe in the
middle. Two pairs of eyes. Not uncommon in streams.

13. **Six-eyed Leech**—*Glossiphonia complanata (L.)*

A broad, flat blood-sucker, about ¾ inch long. Yellow
brown with six rows of small, black dots. Small oral
sucker, the lower one being much larger. The gut is
usually plainly visible. Sucks the blood of snails, especially
Limnaea and *Planorbis*. Mainly in streams.

In most leeches the eggs are attached to stones etc. In this
and the following one there is some brood-care; the eggs are
carried under the body. When the young hatch, they remain
attached to the parent animal for some time.

14. **Two-eyed Leech**—*Helobdella stagnalis (L.)*

Has only one pair of eyes. Body grey with brown spots; at the back of the head is a round light-brown spot. ± ½ inch. Sucks the blood of snails, especially species of *Physa*. Common.

15. **Eight-eyed Leech**—*Herpobdella octoculata (L.)*

Body broad towards the lower part, ending in a large sucker. Head with four pairs of eyes (see fig. 15b). No chitinous 'teeth' in the mouth. Feeds on small worms, water fleas, etc. Colour: brownish; sometimes having two rows of light spots. Common. ± 2 inches.

16. **Horse Leech**—*Haemopsis sanguisuga (L.)*

Body broader towards the hinder end. The hind sucker is half the width of the body. Head with five pairs of eyes; three chitinous 'teeth' in the mouth. Feeds on worms, snails, insect larvae and small fish. Colour: brown-green with darker spots, the lower side lighter. Common. ±2½ inches.

MOSS ANIMALCULES *(Bryozoa)*

These little animals form colonies which at first sight look like polyps. They have not, however, got a simple cavity like the coelenterates nor are they segmented like the worms.

Each animalcule has a crown of tentacles around the mouth. The gut has both stomach and intestine, with an anus, which may be inside or outside the crown of tentacles. (These features can be seen only with the help of a microscope).

There are two sub-divisions called respectively the Entoprocta and the Ectoprocta. The first group includes the moss animalcules found in the sea; the second group contains a number of freshwater forms. In all the freshwater species (including those found in brackish water) the tentacle-crown (or lophophore) is horseshoe-shaped. The animalcules have a chitinous covering into which they can withdraw, and this exo-skeleton of the colony remains when the animal dies.

These sheaths, sometimes called cells, may be separate (fig. 4) but may be attached to each other (fig. 2) or even fused, in which case there is a large cavity into which many animalcules can withdraw. The exo-skeleton is not always stiff and may be slimy. In most of the fresh water species there is a tongue-shaped lid (peristome) over the mouth.

The tentacles set up a water current towards the mouth; one-celled animals or detritus (organic matter) are filtered out for food.

The eggs of these animals hatch out as larvae which swim freely for some time, and on settling each develops into a small colony.

The freshwater Bryozoa produce 'statoblasts', small groups of cells covered by a hard wall, which develop like the gemmules of the sponges. They are much smaller than the gemmules but are also able to resist bad weather conditions. Different species of Bryozoa can be identified by the shape of the statoblasts.

The shape of the colony is not in itself a satisfactory guide to identification; in the descriptions which follow the commonest shape for each species has been given, but it should be remembered that this may vary greatly according to local circumstances.

1. *Plumatella repens v. Ben.*

Colonies formed of tubular branches. The method of growth gives the colony the appearance of creeping. Found on the underside of Water Lily leaves. Dark brown. Common.

Plumatella fungosa (Pall.)
Colonies found on various objects; stones, snail-shells etc. forming a thick layer. The ones on stems form a number of small bumps near each other. The bumps may be about 4

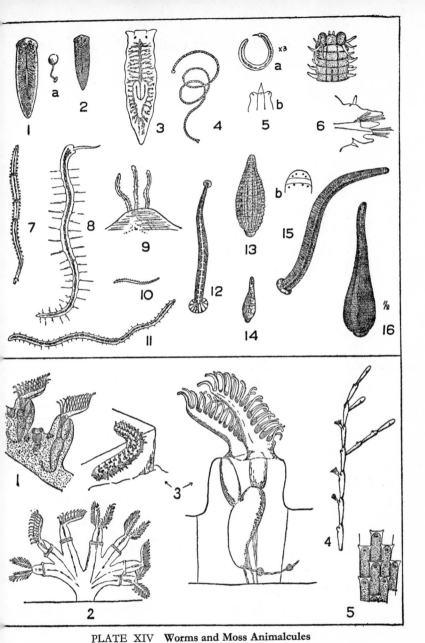

PLATE XIV Worms and Moss Animalcules

WORMS: 1. Brown Flatworm; 2. Black Flatworm; 3. White Flatworm; 4. Hairworm;
5. *Dorylamius stagnalis*; 6. Iridescent Nereis; 7. *Chaetogaster diaphanus*; 8. *Stylaria lacustris*;
9. Tube Worm; 10. White Pot Worm; 11. Brittle Pot Worm; 12. Fish Leech; 13. Six-eyed
Leech; 14. Two-eyed Leech; 15. Eight-eyed Leech; 16. Horse Leech.

MOSS ANIMALCULES: 1. *Plumatella repens*; 2. *Lophopus crystallinus*; 3. *Cristatella mucedo*;
4. *Paludicella ehrenbergii*; 5. *Membranipora membranacea*.

inches in diameter but are usually smaller and about one inch across.

There are many forms intermediate between this and the next species.

2. *Lophopus crystallinus Pall.*

Small colony (—1¾ inches), fan-shaped, with an opaque, light-blue, gelatinous wall. There is a common cavity into which the animals can withdraw. The gut of each animal shines a reddish-brown and each has a yellowish lophophore. Towards the autumn it becomes more liquid and the colony forms a slimy mass in which are the statoblasts.

Fredericella sultana Bl.

Branching colony with almost cylindrical tubes, usually hanging downwards. Inside the wall are all sorts of indigestible remains, such as the skeletons of other animals. The lophophore seems round, but is really horseshoe-shaped with about 20 tentacles.

3. *Cristatella mucedo Cuv.*

Colony long, worm-shaped and about 2 inches long. The wall is very thin; at times it becomes liquid so that the colony slowly moves and eventually forms a slimy smear. The different animals are arranged in successive rows. It forms thick masses on all kinds of objects.

4. *Paludicella ehrenbergii. v. Ben.*

Small colony with projecting branches. Each branch is built up from very small animalcules, one above each other, each about $\frac{1}{25}$ inch long, so that the branch is less than that in thickness. Tentacles in a ring. The branches stand freely in the water or lie against stones, wood etc.

Victorella pavida Kent

Colony long with translucent branches having root-like outgrowths (stolons). Eight tentacles in a ring. Does not form statoblasts for the winter but forms "buds" on the stolons. The brackish water form is found as a velvety layer on shells. This form can be identified by the squarish upper edge of the cells, seen in both old and young animals.

5. *Membranipora membranacea (L.)*

The colony forms a thick crust on stones etc. The cells are right-angled and are arranged in rows, so that it looks like fine gauze. In brackish water.

MOLLUSCS *(Mollusca)*

The empty shells of the sea-molluscs found on the beach are attractive to amateur naturalists because of their colours and forms. Collections of them are often made as they are easy to find and to keep. From such a collection one can get to know a great deal about the shells but not much about the animals themselves. It is not easy to study the sea-molluscs in natural conditions, but it is much simpler to do so with the molluscs of the land and fresh water; and one is also able to follow the development from the egg to the adult in an aquarium.

Less interest is usually shown by amateur naturalists in the freshwater molluscs than in the marine ones. Consequently there is a wide field of study available in which there is the chance of making important scientific discoveries. It is worth noting, however, that such discoveries are valuable only when based on accurate observations, including a careful record of the habitat and geographical position.

There are two main types of molluscs found in fresh and brackish water; first, the snails and second, the bivalves. The commonest kinds are given in the pictures. The related squids are never found in inland waters, only in the sea.

When one studies the snail, the first thing one notices is the shell. There are also 'snails' without shells but they are not found in fresh water, only in the sea or on land. The snail can retreat into its shell and is often able to close the opening with a calcareous or horny plate called the operculum.

The snail shell is usually coiled spirally, mostly twisting to the right when viewed from above, though sometimes to the left. The spirals are usually close to each other and formed in such a way that there is a central tube or columella. This often opens near the mouth of the shell forming a small hole or split, known as the umbilicus. When the spirals lie in one plane, the umbilicus is central. If the spirals are distinct, the grooves between them are called the suture-lines.

When a snail is creeping, one can distinguish a head, with eyes, tentacles and mouth, and also a strong, muscular foot. A special fold of skin, the mantle, forms the shell. Part of the snail, including the intestine, will always be inside the shell cavity together with the greater part of the mantle. Between the mantle and body there is a space known as the mantle-cavity; this plays an important part in the animal's respiration as it may contain gills, or the mantle-cavity itself may become filled with air. In the latter case, the mantle has many branched blood-vessels and the oxygen is quickly absorbed from the air into the blood. The air in the mantle-cavity has to be renewed, so these 'lung-snails' have to go to the surface at regular intervals.

Nos. 1 to 9 are all "gill-snails"; nos. 10 to 33 are "lung-snails".

Sometimes the mantle can be partly protruded and turned up against the shell (accessory gill). The blood in this part can absorb the oxygen dissolved in the water.

By contractions of the foot a creeping movement is effected. When there is an operculum it can be seen, in the moving animal, posteriorly on the foot.

On the head is a pair of tentacles. There are two eyes which, in the freshwater snails, are on the bases of the tentacles.

In the mouth is the radula, or rasping tongue, a structure bearing rows of chitinous 'teeth'. The shape and position of these teeth are characteristic of each species and can be used for identification.

The bivalves have, of course, double shells, the two halves being attached together by a central hinge and ligament. This is a strong, elastic structure which effects the opening of the shell-valves. The shell is closed by strong muscles. In the freshwater bivalves there are two of these, but in some marine forms, like the oyster, there is only one. On the inside of the empty shell can be seen the places to which the muscles were attached, as they leave rough marks on the surface. The hinge often has toothed projections which fit into grooves when the shell is closed, making a strong joint. The shape and structure of this 'lock' can be used to distinguish between the different species of bivalves.

The body of these animals has a strongly, muscular foot and two skin folds forming the mantle which lies on the inside of the shell valves and secretes them. As the animal grows, more material is added at the margins of the valves and consequently growth-lines are visible. This is also to be seen in the snails. In the mantle-cavity, between the mantle and the foot, there are two plate-like gills on each side. The water enters posteriorly and passes through the mantle-cavity so that the oxygen is extracted as it passes over the gills. At the same time food particles are filtered out and directed, by cilia, to the mouth. The water leaves by an excurrent opening. Both openings lie close together. Sometimes the mantle has a tubular outgrowth so that these openings are carried a distance from the shell. Such a tube is called a siphon. It can be withdrawn into the shell. It is valuable in bivalves which lie partly buried in the mud.

The shell is made of three layers. The outermost is the epidermis made of conchine. This is an organic substance, rather like horn, which may have disappeared from empty shells. The second layer and the innermost layers are both calcareous and inorganic. The innermost is called mother-of-pearl and is prettily coloured, as it refracts light. Thus a mollusc shell is made of lime and conchine; it is the latter which is the more important and gives the shell its colour.

In the following descriptions the colour of the shell is always given, but shells are often covered by a brown or black encrustation, so that the real colour cannot be seen.

(i) GILL SNAILS *(Operculates)*

1. **Freshwater Nerite**—*Theodoxus fluviatilis* (L.)

   The lowest whorl of the shell is very large, while the other whorls are relatively very small. Colour: white or brownish with dark red or black mottling. Columella inside and not visible. No umbilicus. Operculum (see drawing) calcareous with a tooth-like projection, which grips the edge of the columella when the shell is closed. $\frac{1}{5} — \frac{2}{5} \times \frac{1}{2}$ inch.[1] Foot yellow-red with black flecks.

   Common in fresh and brackish water on stones etc., in rivers and canals, found mostly in the south.
   (Neritina fluviatilis)

2. **Freshwater Winkle**—*Viviparus viviparus (L.)*

   Sturdy, yellow, brown or greenish shell with flattened whorls, usually having one faint and two clear reddish-brown spiral bands on it. Top blunt. Umbilicus hidden. $1\frac{2}{5} \times 1\frac{1}{5}$ inches. Operculum present. Viviparous. The young animals have usually, for a few days, long hairs on the shell.

   Common in rivers and lakes as far north as Yorkshire.
   (Paludina vivipara)

3. **River Snail**—*Viviparus lacustris Beck.*

   Sturdy, yellow, brown or greenish shell with bulbous whorls, usually having one faint and two clear red-brown spiral bands. The last whorl is about half the total height. Top with a sharp point. Umbilicus clearly visible. $1\frac{4}{5} \times 1\frac{2}{5}$ inches. Body dark grey with yellow spots.
   North to Yorkshire.
   (Viviparus fasciatus) (Paludina contecta)

---

[1] The measurements relate to the shells. Therefore $\frac{1}{5} — \frac{2}{5} \times \frac{1}{2}$ means $\frac{1}{5}$ to $\frac{2}{5}$ inch high and $\frac{1}{2}$ inch wide.

4. **Common Valve Snail**—*Valvata piscinalis (Müll.)*

   Shell dark brown or greenish, shiny, with fine cross-markings. Umbilicus distinct and circular. $\frac{1}{4} \times \frac{1}{2}$ inch.

   All the Valve Snails have a feathery gill on the right side, projecting from under the shell.

   Common in still and slow-moving water, especially at the edges of lakes.

5. **Large-mouthed Valve Snail**—*Valvata pulchella Stud.*

   Shell yellow-brown, yellow-green or horny coloured, shiny, having fine transverse lines. Umbilicus distinct. $\frac{1}{5} \times \frac{1}{4}$ inch. See also no. 4.

   Fairly common in England in the south, east and the Midlands.

   (Valvata macrostoma St.)

6. **Flat Valve Snail**—*Valvata cristata Müll.*

   Shell brown-yellow with fine cross markings. The shell mouth is circular and its edge is entire. (See *Planorbis* in a later description). Whorls cylindrical with distinct suture-lines. Large umbilicus. $\frac{1}{16} \times \frac{1}{3}$ inch.

   Found in streams and ditches among close-growing plants. Not very common.

7. **Common Bithynia**—*Bithynia tentaculata (L.)*

   Shell yellow or greenish-brown, sometimes grey; shiny. Suture lines only shallow. Umbilicus hidden, sometimes seen as a groove. $\frac{4}{5} \times \frac{2}{5}$ inch.

   Fairly common. In still and slow-moving water throughout the British Isles. May be found in brackish water.

8. **Leach's Bithynia**—*Bithynia leachii (Shepp.)*

   Shell yellow or greyish brown; shiny. Distinct suture lines. Umbilicus hidden, sometimes like a groove. $\frac{2}{5} \times \frac{1}{4}$ inch.

   Fairly common in the south and Midlands. May be found in brackish water.

Jenkin's Spire Shell—*Paludestrina jenkinsi (Smith)*

Shell yellowish-brown or yellowish-green, turret-shaped with six to seven rather bulbous whorls, the last being the largest and most bulbous. Deep sutures. Sometimes the last whorl has a keel, and in some forms there is a row of short projections. Viviparous. $\frac{1}{4} \times \frac{1}{8}$ inch.

In fresh and brackish water. Has recently spread over the country from the sea and is now common. A drawing is given in *Plants and Animals of the Seashore*, page 53.
(*Hydrobia jenkinsi*) (*Potamopyrgus jenkinsi*)

9. *Lithoglyphus naticoides (Fér.)*

Shell yellowish or yellow-green, not shiny. Sutures shallow. No umbilicus. In the ♂ the outer edge of the shell mouth is protruded, in the ♀ this edge is straight.

Chiefly in large rivers and lakes, not in brackish water. Not recorded in Great Britain.

(ii) **LUNG SNAILS *(Pulmonates)***

10. **River Limpet**—*Ancylus fluviatilis Müll.*

Shell thin, cap-shaped, not having much lime in it. At the base it is broadly oval. Horn coloured or yellow-grey; inside white or pearly. $\frac{1}{8} \times \frac{1}{4}$ inch, may lengthen to $\frac{2}{8}$ inch. Grey body with black spots on the edge of the mantle.

Common in moving fresh water all over Britain.
(*Ancylastrum fluviatile*)

11. **Lake Limpet**—*Acroloxus lacustris (L.)*

Shell yellowish, also thin (like no. 10), cap-shaped. The base is a narrow oval. $\frac{1}{10} \times \frac{1}{5}$ inch, lengthening to $\frac{2}{8}$ inch. The body is dark grey or greenish and has no black spots on the mantle-edge.

Common in south and Midlands, in slow-moving water, usually on water plants.
(*Ancylus lacustris*)

12. **Ram's Horn Snail**—*Planorbis corneus (L.)*

Shell red-brown, dark grey or greenish yellow with distinct growth lines. Shell mouth broadly sickle-shaped, edge sharp. Cylindrical whorls getting gradually larger. $\frac{3}{8} \times \frac{2}{8}$ inch. When the animal moves an outgrowth of the mantle can be seen (accessory gill, see page 62). The young animal has a hairy shell.

Common mostly in the south-east and the Midlands.

In the *Planorbis* species the shell mouth is always obliquely half-moon-shaped and the edge is usually not entire. The top of the shell does not project outside the flattened whorls. The shell has a left-handed twist. In contrast with other snails these animals have a red pigment (haemoglobin) in their blood, which combines readily with oxygen.

13. **Common Trumpet Snail**—*Planorbis planorbis (L.)*

The last whorl of the shell has an indistinct keel, under the mid-line. The horn-coloured or brown shell is flat underneath and somewhat bulbous above. At the same time the last whorl is somewhat flattened by the opening. $\frac{1}{5} \times \frac{4}{5}$ inch.

Common in still, fresh water or sometimes in slightly brackish water. *(Tropidoniscus planorbis)*

14. **Keeled Trumpet Snail**—*Planorbis carinatus Müll.*

The last whorl of the brown shell has a distinct, narrow keel which is exactly on the mid-line. The whorls get rapidly larger. Edge of shell mouth entire. $\frac{1}{8} \times \frac{4}{5}$ inch.

Common in slow-moving water in most parts of the British Isles. *(Tropidoniscus carinatus)*

15. **Whirlpool Trumpet Snail**—*Planorbis vortex (L.)*

The yellow-brown shell is flat and sharply keeled. The underside is flat and the upper side is higher at the sides than in the centre. $\frac{1}{10} \times \frac{1}{2}$ inch.

Common in fresh and slightly brackish water. *(Spiralina vortex)*

16. **Round-spired Trumpet Snail**—*Planorbis leucostoma Millet*
    The light-brown shell has whorls which become slowly larger and only an indistinct keel. $\frac{1}{16} \times \frac{2}{5}$ inch.
    (Planorbis spirorbis (L.))
    Generally distributed, rarer in Scotland.

17. **Twisted Trumpet Snail**—*Planorbis contortus (L.)*
    Light or dark brown shell with small whorls becoming slowly larger, without a keel. The underside has a large umbilicus and the upper side is flat. $\frac{1}{10} \times \frac{2}{5}$ inch.
    Common in standing fresh and slightly brackish water. *(Bathyomphalus contortus)*

18. **White Trumpet Snail**—*Planorbis albus Müll.*
    The small, cream-coloured shell has a large final whorl with a broad, sickle-shaped opening. The surface is marked by a lattice-work of radiating and spiral striations. $\frac{1}{10} \times \frac{1}{5}$ inch.
    Common in ponds. *(Gyraulus albus)*

19. **Nautilus Trumpet Snail**—*Planorbis crista (L.)*
    A grey or light brown shell with two to three whorls, the last being the largest. Usually with radiating ridges and small prickles along the outer edge. Shell mouth edge not entire. Underside concave, with indistinct umbilicus, upperside flat. $\frac{1}{50} \times \frac{1}{8}$ inch.
    Widespread.
    (Armiger crista) (Planorbis nautileus (L.))

20. **Flat Trumpet Snail**—*Planorbis complanatus (L.)*
    A very shiny, horn-coloured shell of three to four whorls, the first ones being very coiled. Strongly keeled. $\frac{1}{16} \times \frac{1}{5}$ inch.

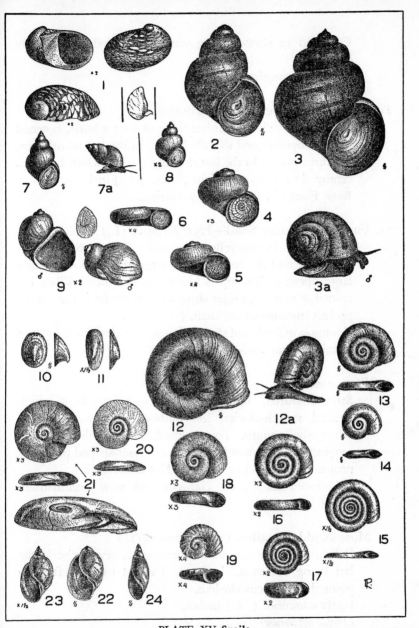

PLATE XV **Snails**

1. Freshwater Nerite; 2. Freshwater Winkle; 3. River Snail; 4. Common Valve Snail;
5. Large-mouthed Valve Snail; 6. Flat Valve Snail; 7. Common Bithynia; 8. Leach's Bithynia;
9. *Lithoglyphus naticoides*; 10. River Limpet; 11. Lake Limpet; 12. Ram's Horn Snail; 13.
Common Trumpet Snail; 14. Keeled Trumpet Snail; 15. Whirlpool Trumpet Snail; 16.
Round-spired Trumpet Snail; 17. Twisted Trumpet Snail; 18. White Trumpet Snail;
19. Nautilus Trumpet Snail; 20. Flat Trumpet Snail; 21. Shining Trumpet Snail; 22. Fountain Bladder Snail; 23. *Physa acuta*; 24. Moss Bladder Snail.

Common in slow-running water, both fresh and slightly
brackish.
(Hippeutis complanatus)

21. **Shining Trumpet Snail**—*Segmentina nitida (Müll.)*
   The brown-yellow shell has three to four whorls, fastened
   closely together and slightly keeled. In the last whorl there
   are three plates. In the last drawing the last whorl has been
   removed to show one of the plates. $\frac{1}{16} \times \frac{1}{4}$ inch.
   Rare. Found in a few marshy districts.

22. **Fountain Bladder Snail**—*Physa fontinalis (L.)*
   The shiny, brown-yellow, opaque shell is coiled anti-
   clockwise and the last whorl is large and bulbous, with a
   large opening. The tip is blunt. No umbilicus. When the
   animal is moving, finger-shaped processes from the mantle
   project from under the shell. $\frac{2}{5} \times \frac{2}{5}$ inch.
   Common in fresh and slightly brackish water. Lives in clean
   running water among plants.

23. *Physa acuta Drap.*
   Straw-coloured, light-brown or greenish-yellow shell,
   twisted anti-clockwise, less bulbous and more slender.
   Large shell-mouth. Top pointed. No umbilicus. When
   moving the two mantle folds have finger-shaped processes
   projecting from below the shell. Not common.
   Introduced into Kew Gardens and now acclimatised.
   $\frac{3}{5} \times \frac{2}{5}$ inch.

24. **Moss Bladder Snail**—*Aplecta hypnorum (L.)*
   Polished, brown, opaque shell with six to seven whorls, the
   last being somewhat bulbous. Twisted to the left. Top
   pointed. Umbilicus slit-like.
   Fairly common. $\frac{2}{5} \times \frac{1}{5}$ inches.
   (Physa hypnorum)

25. **Greater Pond Snail**—*Limnaea stagnalis (L.)*

Shell horn-coloured, marked by growth-lines, pointed top. Last whorl large. Shell mouth pointed at the top. No umbilicus.

Common in large ponds and slow rivers. $2\frac{3}{8} \times 1\frac{2}{8}$ inches. Also found in slightly brackish water.

Wandering Snail *Limnaea pereger*.

Commonest British water snail. Smaller than no. 25. Less pointed, though shell shape varies. Shell mouth large.

26. **Ear-shaped Pond Snail**—*Limnaea auricularia (L.)*

A brown shell which is shorter than no. 25, the shell mouth is ear-shaped. Pointed top.

Common in fresh water, mostly in the south and east. $1\frac{1}{8} \times 1$ inches.

27. **Oval Pond Snail**—*Limnaea ovata (Drap.)*

Brown—yellow short, turret-shaped shell with large opening. Top less pointed than no. 26. Four to five whorls, with the last much larger than the others. $1 \times \frac{4}{5}$ inches.

Found in fresh and brackish water.

28. **Bog Snail**—*Limnaea palustris (Müll.)*

Dark brown, turret-shaped shell, taller than no. 27, with seven to eight whorls. The last two whorls are largest. The inner edge of the shell-mouth is chestnut-brown. $1\frac{1}{8} \times \frac{3}{8}$ inches.

Not very common. Found in bogs.

29. **Dwarfed Limnaea**—*Limnaea truncatula (Müll.)*

Shell brown, cone-shaped and strong, with five distinct bulbous whorls. $\frac{2}{8} \times \frac{1}{8}$ inches.

Found in fresh and brackish water, sometimes on marshy land.

(This snail is frequently the host of the larval stage of the Liver-fluke. *Fasciola hepatica (L.)* The adult flukes live in the liver of sheep and cause disease.)

30. **Smooth Pond Snail**—*Limnaea glabra (Müll.)*
Brown, smooth, small shell forming a tall turret with seven to eight whorls, which are not very bulbous.
$\frac{2}{8} \times \frac{1}{8}$ inches.
In marshy grass near water and ponds, sometimes temporary ones. Rare.

31. **Glutinous Snail**—*Myxas glutinosa (Müll.)*
The lowest whorl is large and surrounds the other two. Edge of the shell mouth not entire. No umbilicus. $\frac{4}{5} \times \frac{3}{5}$ inches. The body is grey with small, light spots and has a black-flecked mantle.
Rare.

32. **Large Amber Snail**—*Succinea putris (L.)*
The lowest whorl is large and swollen, above are two to three small whorls. The shell can be recognised by its opening; the point of the lowest whorl is above the level of the upper whorls. Colour: yellow or light brown. Sutures deep. Mouth oblique and greater than half the height. Varies in shape. $1\frac{1}{10} \times \frac{3}{5}$ inches.
Found in southern parts of British Isles.

33. **Pfeiffer's Amber Shell**—*Succinea pfeifferi Rossm.*
Shell brown-yellow, mouth somewhat oblique. The upper edge of the mouth is protruded over the lower edge. The lowest of the three to four whorls is larger than all the others together. When the shell is placed mouth down on a flat surface, the top whorls project above the bottom whorl. Opening more than half the height. $\frac{2}{8} \times \frac{2}{8}$ inches.
Common.

(iii) BIVALVES *(Lamellibranchiates)*

34. **Swan Mussel**—*Anodonta cygnea var. zellensis (Gmel.)*
Shell valves very thin, without a "lock". Rather oblong-

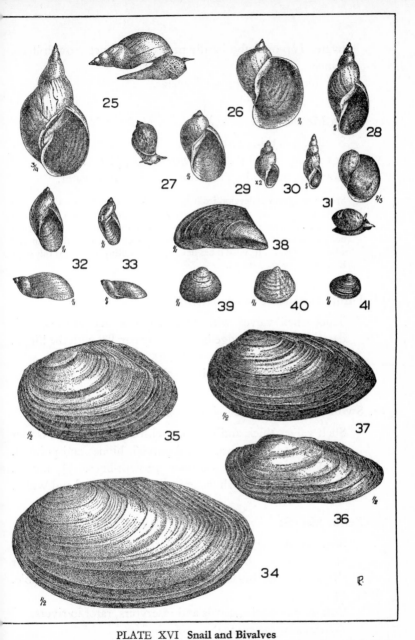

PLATE XVI Snail and Bivalves

25. Greater Pond Snail; 26. Ear-shaped Pond Snail; 27. Oval Pond Snail; 28. Bog Snail;
29. Dwarfed Limnaea; 30. Smooth Pond Snail; 31. Glutinous Snail; 32. Large Amber
Snail; 33. Pfeiffer's Amber Snail; 34-35. Two varieties of Swan Mussel; 36. Painter's
Mussel; 37. Swollen River Mussel; 38. Zebra Mussel; 39. Horny Orb-shell Cockle; 40. Lake
Orb-shell Cockle; 41. River Pea-shell Cockle.

ovate. Top or umbo hardly projects. Distinct growth lines.
6 inches.
Common in standing fresh water.

35. Swan Mussel—*Anodonta cygnea var. piscinalis Nills.*

Shell valves thin, without a "lock". Ovate in shape—shorter than no. 34. Distinct growth lines. 4 inches.
Common in standing and slow moving fresh water.

Species of *Anodonta* develop from eggs which are carried between the gills of the parent animal and hatch as larvae. These larvae have two valves with teeth and a byssus thread which sticks out and by means of which they become attached to fishes. The larva then burrows through the skin and adopts a parasitic life, until it has developed into a tiny mussel. At this stage it drops off to the bottom.

36. Painter's Mussel—*Unio pictorum (L.)*

Thick shell valves with a strong lock and greenish epidermis. The lower edge is practically parallel with the hinge. Growth lines very clear. 3½ inches.
Common in fresh water in England and Wales.

37. Swollen River Mussel—*Unio tumidus Retz.*

Shell valves thick and bulbous with a strong hinge. Under edge curved, front broad and curved, hinder end pointed. Epidermis greenish. Distinct growth-lines. 3½ inches.
Common in clear fresh water in parts of England and Wales.

38. Zebra Mussel—*Dreissena polymorpha (Pall.)*

Shell valves definitely triangular. Attached in groups to various objects by sticky byssus threads. The triangular shape and the byssus threads make it easily identifiable. 1½ inches.
Common in docks, canals and reservoirs, rarer in rivers.
(Dreissensia polymorpha)

39. **Horny Orb-shell Cockle**—*Sphaerium corneum (L.)*

Shells yellow or brown, globular, point or umbo central. ½ inch.

Lives at the bottom of standing water. Common.

40. **Lake Orb-shell Cockle**—*Musculium lacustre (Müll.)*

Thin shells, top rather tubular and projecting centrally. ½ inch.

In streams, pools and lakes with muddy bottoms. Not very common. *(Sphaerium lacustre)*

41. **River Pea Shell Cockle**—*Pisidium amnicum (Müll.)*

Flat shells, the umbo is nearer the back. Distinct growth lines. ± ⅛ inch.

Common in streams, ponds, rivers etc. mostly in running water.

The species of *Pisidium* are difficult to separate. There are many of them (15 in Britain) varying from ⅛ to ½ inch in diameter.

CRUSTACEANS *(Crustacea)*

The Crustaceans belong to the Arthropoda, which, as the name implies, have jointed legs. This group includes the Spiders and the Insects, but in these animals there are no legs on the abdomen, as there are in the Crustaceans. The body is also jointed, though this is not always obvious. The crabs and shrimps are jointed: although there is a fused cephalo-thorax (i.e. they have no 'neck'), the abdomen is clearly jointed. The cephalo-thorax provides a good protection for the body and the gills lie beneath it.

The carapace, or exoskeleton, is made of chitin and in the larger animals this is reinforced by calcareous deposits, so that it is very strong. In some species, e.g. the water-fleas, the carapace is thin and transparent, and the body is enclosed in two separate valves which protect the body and the legs. The head, with the branched antennae, is outside.

The carapace is not elastic and has to be shed at intervals as the body grows. The smaller crustaceans, e.g. the water-fleas, the fish lice etc., are not easily recognised as such, as the segmentation is not clear. They can be identified by the shape of the larva (the nauplius) as this is typical of these animals.

The crustaceans breathe by means of gills, which are attached at the bases of the legs and are protected under the carapace. Special appendages cause the water, carrying dissolved oxygen, to stream over the gills.

Many of the smaller crustaceans merely float in the water, without swimming properly, and form a considerable portion of the plankton (a collection of small plants and animals which can scarcely be seen except through a microscope). This provides food for larger animals like fish. The plankton contains an enormous number of different species of both plants and animals and it is impossible to identify them all. This book gives only the commoner ones.

1. **Freshwater Crayfish**—*Astacus astacus (L.)*
   (Potamobius fluviatilis Fabr.)
   The picture shows an animal, about 6 inches long, which is very easy to recognise. Lives in rivers, mostly in a hole in the bank. Common locally, especially in Kent and Hertfordshire.
   A smaller species *(Potamobius pallipes)* may also be found in Great Britain.

2. **Chinese Crab**— *Eriocheir sinensis M. Edw.*
   The pincers bear a "muff" formed by a thick mass of long hairs which makes this animal easy to identify. The carapace is nearly 4 inches across and 3 inches long. Harmful, as it destroys fishing nets.
   Introduced to Germany from China in 1911. (The larvae live in the sea, therefore it is possible that the species will be found in Great Britain).

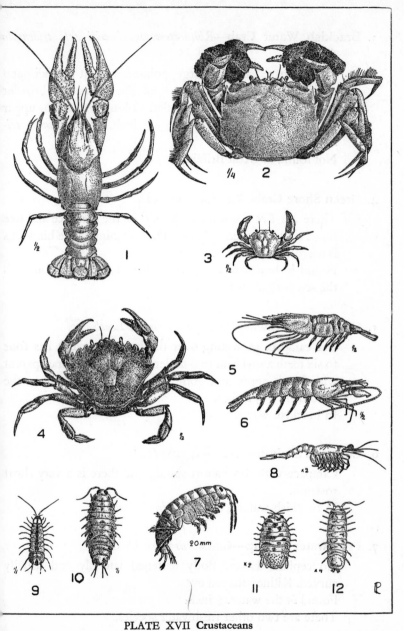

PLATE XVII Crustaceans

. Freshwater Crayfish; 2. Chinese Crab; 3. Brackish Water Crab; 4. Green Shore Crab;
. Chameleon Prawn; 6. Common Shrimp; 7. Freshwater Shrimp; 8. Shrimp; 9. Water Hog
Louse; 10. Sea Slater; 11. Water Louse; 12. White-headed Louse.

3. **Brackish Water Crab**—*Rhithropanopeus harrisi ssp. tridentata (Maitl.)*

> The carapace has three large, pointed teeth at the sides and one indentation between the eyes. The carapace is broader than its length and is rather flat. Colour: brownish, upper side marbled red or green. $\pm$ $\frac{3}{8}$ inch. (*Heteropanope tridentata Maitl.*)
>
> Not found in Great Britain.

4. **Green Shore Crab**—*Carcinus meanas L.*

> There are five teeth on each side of the carapace and five blunt teeth between the eyes. The last joint of the hind-legs is narrow and pointed.
>
> Found in brackish water when there is a connection with the sea.—$1\frac{3}{4}$ inches.

5. **Chameleon Prawn**—*Palaemonetes varians Leach*

> The carapace projecting over the head (rostrum) has four to six teeth above and two underneath. Colour: transparent with black spots and some orange-yellow flecks on the abdomen. $\pm$ $\frac{1}{2}$ inches.
>
> In brackish water.

6. **Common Shrimp**—*Crangon crangon (L.)*

> Carapace with three short spines, and there is a very short rostrum.
>
> In brackish water. (*Crangon vulgaris Fabr.*)

7. **Freshwater Shrimp**—*Gammarus pulex De G.*

> No cephalo-thorax. Body flattened laterally and usually curved. Kidney-shaped eyes.
>
> Found *in* the water. $\frac{3}{4}$ inch.
>
> There are two other freshwater species.

Shore-skipper—*Orchestia gammarellus (Pall.)*
Second pair of thoracic legs with large "hands" as long as
they are broad. Round eyes. Colour: greenish.
On the land among stones at the water's edge. ± ½ inch.

8. **Shrimp**—*Neomysis vulgaris (Thomps.)*
   Cephalo-thorax with long legs; the small abdomen has only
   undeveloped legs (except for the last pair which form the
   first part of the tail-fin). The legs are typically two-branched,
   consisting of a basal joint with two branches. On the back
   there are x-shaped marks. Colour: greenish.
   Mostly in brackish water. — ¾ inch.
   (Neomysis integer (Leach))

9. **Water Hog Louse**—*Asellus aquaticus L.*
   Body in distinct segments. The last segment is three times
   the length of previous one (due to fusion of three segments).
   Two small eyes. Colour: greenish-brown.
   Common. ± ½ inch. ♂ larger than the ♀.

10. **Sea Slater**—*Ligia oceanica L.*
    The last abdominal segment has two teeth. Colour: greenish.
    In brackish water. ± 1⅛ inch.

11. **Water Louse**—*Sphaeroma rugicauda Leach*
    Last abdominal segment has two projections and two large,
    flat legs. At the least sign of danger it rolls itself up. Colour:
    greyish with dark spots.
    In brackish water. ± ⅔ inch.

12. **White-headed Louse**—*Jaera albifrons Leach*
    The last segment has no projections. The front of the head
    is white. Colour: greyish with irregular brown markings.
    In brackish water. ± ⅛ inch.

13. **Cyclops**—*Cyclops viridis Jur.*

A plankton animal about $\frac{1}{10}$ inch long. The antennae are shorter than the thorax. Small abdomen ending in a long, forked tail. Two egg-sacs. The animals move jerkily in the water.

There are many species of Cyclops. They can be identified by the shape of the fifth pair of legs which are undeveloped (rudimentary).

14. *Diaptomus gracilis Sars.*

A plankton animal, about $\frac{1}{10}$ inch long. Antennae longer than the body, serving to keep it afloat. Cephalo-thorax long, broader and longer than the abdomen. Only one egg sac.

Found in ponds in the summer. The related species *Diaptomus castor* is commonly found in ponds in the winter.

15. *Eurytemora affinis (Poppe)*

A plankton animal, $\frac{1}{15}$ th. inch long. Antennae rather shorter than the cephalo-thorax, which is long. The last segment is broad and wing-shaped. One egg-sac.

16. **Fish Louse**—*Argulus foliaceus L.*

A plankton animal. $\frac{2}{8}$ inch. The carapace covers the head and 1 thoracic segment, it is somewhat heart-shaped and to it are attached the other thoracic segments and also a short unsegmented abdomen. Two eyes. On the underside are two suckers. The animals feed by sucking the blood of fishes, usually sticklebacks. No egg-sacs; the eggs are deposited in rows on stones, etc.

17. **Water Flea**—*Daphnia magna Strauss*

A plankton animal about $\frac{1}{4}$ inch. Carapace is thin and transparent, and covers the whole animal except for the head.

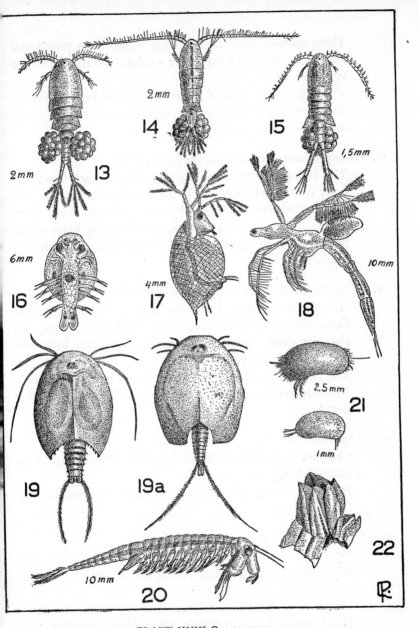

PLATE XVIII **Crustaceans**

13. Cyclops; 14. *Diaptomus gracilis*; 15. *Eurytemora affenis*; 16. Fish Louse; 17. Water Flea;
18. Glassy Water Flea; 19. Crab Shield Scrimp; 19a. *Lepidurus apus*; 20. *Branchipus
schaefferi*; 21. Ostracods; 22. Brackish Water Barnacle.

These animals are found in large numbers in ponds and streams; so that they may form a thick brown layer on the surface.

There are many kinds of *Daphnia*, they may be identified by the shape of the abdomen, the appearance of the single eye and the shape of the head and carapace.

18. **Glassy Water Flea**—*Leptodora hyalina Lill.*

This transparent plankton animal is about ⅔ inch long. The body is long, with a few cylindrical segments. On the back is a brood-pouch formed by the carapace. Very large antennae and six pairs of legs, all with long hairs which help it to float. Eats other plankton animals. *(Leptodora kindtii F.)*

19. **Crab Shield Shrimp**—*Apus cancriformis Bosc.*

A large, flat carapace. From the back can be seen only the three swim-bristles of each of the first pair of legs, and also the short, segmented abdomen with two long tail-filaments. Three eyes.

May be found in temporary pools formed by rain. ± 1 inch. Not very common. Males very rare. *(Triops cancriformis Bosc.)*

19a. *Lepidurus apus (L.)*

Carapace indented on the hind-end. The swim-bristles are shorter than in no. 19.

In pools. March and April. ± 1 inch. Not recorded in Great Britain.

20. *Branchipus schaefferi Fischer*

No carapace. Body is divided into many segments, each with leaf-shaped appendages. The 9 abdominal segments are without legs. ± ⅜ inch.

Found in similar places to no. 19 and is eaten by it as food. Not recorded in Great Britain. *(Branchipus stagnalis L.)*

21. Ostracods.

The carapace is in the form of two valves, which enclose the animal, so that all that can be seen are the seven pairs of segmented limbs and one pair of long antennae, all of which can be withdrawn. The carapace is calcareous. The whole organism resembles a tiny mussel.

These animals *(Ostracoda)* are difficult to distinguish and therefore no attempt has been made here to list them separately.

22. Brackish Water Barnacle—*Balanus improvisus Darw.*

The epidermis of this animal secretes calcareous plates to surround it. The slender legs project from the case and by their movement direct a water current which carries tiny food particles towards the mouth. The case can be closed by two double opercular plates. The base of the case is chalky and perforated. It is attached to stones, piles, crabs etc. There are other species in the sea. The plates are smooth, except two of the opercular plates which have a deep groove. It is up to $\frac{4}{5}$ inch high at the centre. Found in estuaries.

INSECTS *(Insecta)*

All insects have certain points in common. The body is divided into three distinct regions: the head, the thorax and the abdomen. The head bears a pair of antennae, a pair of large compound eyes (sometimes small eye-spots as well), and—invariably—mouth-parts.

The antennae, the eyes and the mouth-parts, however, may differ very much in the different kinds of insects. These can often be used to classify insects within a particular group. It is usual to name the mouth-parts by reference to the food and feeding habits of the animal. We can distinguish biting mouth-parts (beetles); stabbing and sucking (gnats); licking (bees) and sucking (butterflies).

The thorax always consists of three segments. Each segment

bears a pair of legs and the second and third segments may each have a pair of wings.

The abdomen does not bear any legs, but many have some appendages, for example an ovipositor, a sting or tail filaments.

The flies and gnats have only a single pair of wings, the second pair being represented by balancers.

The beetles have the front pair converted to horny wing-cases and in the resting position, these hide most of the abdomen.

In the bugs only the top halves of the upper wings are leathery, the rest is as membranous as the lower wings; these insects are therefore called the *Hemiptera* (half winged).

When we look at the dorsal view of a beetle, we see: (*a*) the head, (*b*) the first segment of the thorax (prothorax), (*c*) a small portion of the second thoracic segment (mesothorax) and (*d*) the wing-covers hiding the rest of the body.

Insects often lay their eggs on plants. From the egg hatches a larva, which may develop directly into the adult animal (imago) or may first be of a very different form. The larvae always shed their skins several times. In the first group the larva gradually changes to the adult; it grows wings and becomes larger (imperfect metamorphosis). In the second group there is true metamorphosis and each life-history shows the following stages: larva, pupa and adult animal. The moulting of the larva finishes when it pupates. The pupa is a resting stage, but internally important changes are taking place. In many gnats the pupa is found in water; it moves by jerking movements of the abdomen. Mayflies at the stage corresponding to the pupa of other insects, however, can fly like the adult.

Breathing is effected by tracheae. These are fine branching tubes which penetrate right into the organs of the body. Small openings in the body-wall (spiracles) lead into these tubes and connect them with the outer air. By this method atmospheric oxygen is conveyed directly to the organs.

In the aquatic insects air-bubbles are often caught among the hairs under the wings so that the air is in contact with the spiracles. The larvae often have tracheal gills. These are thin folds of skin, usually on the abdomen, inside which are fine branching tracheae; thus gases can be exchanged through the thin skin. Oxygen passes in from the water and carbon dioxide is passed out.

In the plates, for convenience, two other groups of animals, the Water Spiders and the Water Mites, have been included with the Insects. These differ from the insects in having a cephalo-thorax (the head and the thorax are fused), an unsegmented abdomen and four pairs of legs.

Insects offer a wide field for specialist study. The plates in this book show a few larvae, and of the adult insects only those which are easy to recognise or are representatives of a special group are included. The descriptions give only the points by which they may most easily be recognised. Most of the larvae can best be studied in an aquarium.

INSECT LARVAE

1. **Larva of the Great Diving Beetle**—*Dytiscus marginalis* L.
   Distinct, flat head with two pincer-shaped, piercing jaws. Body in distinct segments, pointed at the end and bearing two strong, hairy tail-filaments. Three pairs of thoracic legs each having *two claws*. Breathes by tracheae, which lead to the spiracles on the last abdominal segment. These spiracles are raised to the surface of the water for air to be taken in.

   When prey is seized, it is rapidly pierced by the jaws and injected with a brown fluid, which kills it and digests the organs, so that they can be sucked in by the animal. When the soluble parts have been eaten the empty skin of the prey is dropped from the jaws. Pupation takes place *in* the bank.

   Larva of the Silver Water Beetle—*Hydrous piceus* L.
   Like no. 1 but fatter and slower. Distinct head with pincer like jaws. Three pairs of thoracic legs, on each of which

there is only *one claw*. On the abdomen are two small tail-filaments. Feeds mainly on snails. The prey is not sucked immediately but is first crushed in the jaws. Pupates in the bank.

2. **Larva of the Whirligig Beetle**—*Gyrinus sp.*

Body long and narrow, in distinct segments. The jaws are hollow but not so strong. Three pairs of thoracic legs. Each of the abdominal segments has a pair of tracheal gills; the last segment has two pairs.

To pupate the larva creeps on to a plant above the water, spins a cocoon, which is pointed at both ends, and fastens it to the plant.

3. **Larva and pupa of the Mosquito (Gnat)**—*Culex sp.*

The larva is distinctly segmented. The last segment has two tracheal gills, the previous one having a long breathing tube. Each segment has long bristly hairs. The larva hangs vertically in the water, with the opening of the breathing tube at the surface, while the mouth searches for food. The whole body can be withdrawn below the water.

The pupa has a large cephalo-thorax with two breathing tubes and a curved, jointed abdomen. By movements of the abdomen the pupa can retreat to deeper water. The eggs of the mosquito are laid in groups which float on the water.

4. **Larva of the Malaria Mosquito**—*Anopheles maculipennis Meig.*
The larva is like no. 3 but without the breathing tube. It hangs horizontally with the bristles on the surface.
The pupa is like the previous one. The eggs float separately under the surface.

5. **Larva of the Phantom Midge**—*Chaoborus plumicornis F.*
Very transparent and therefore difficult to see. It is carnivorous. The prey is seized by the prehensile antennae and the

strong jaws. The body is in distinct segments and there is a group of short hairs on each joint. The last segment has a number of stiff hairs which act as a rudder. On both the third and the 10th segments can be seen a pair of air-bladders, which enable the larva to lie horizontally in the water. Respiration takes place through the skin.

6. **Larva of the Midge**—*Chironomus plumosus (L.)*

   Body made up of distinct, cylindrical segments. Head small, with eyespots. Each segment has some small bristles; the first and last segments having unsegmented appendages with many hairs. Respiration is through the skin and there is red-coloured blood. On the abdominal segments there are four tubular outgrowths, which act as gills.

   These larvae often build themselves mud-tubes, while other species live parasitically, e.g. on snails.

   (Tendipus plumosus)

7. **Larva of the Chameleon Fly**—*Stratiomys sp.*

   Brown, segmented larva, without legs (a maggot), pointed at each end. The body rather broad. At the anterior end are the mouth parts and toothed bristles, which the animal uses to move about in the mud. There is a breathing tube on the abdomen, the opening of which is surrounded by fine hairs; by this an air bubble can be drawn into the water. When the larva comes to the surface, it spreads these hairs out on the surface. The animal hangs with its head just underneath. Pupation takes place within the skin of the larva.

8. **Larva of the Drone Fly (Rat-tailed Maggot)**— *Eristalomyia tenax L.*

   A cylindrical, segmented larva with a very long breathing tube. 7 pairs of "legs" with chitinous hooks. The head is not distinct. The long retractable breathing tube is responsible for the name of "rat-tailed". The pupa forms inside the larval skin.

   (Eristalis tenax L.)

9. Larva of the Caddis Fly (Caddis Worm)—*Phryganea sp.*

The larva builds a tube out of pieces of plant or other substances, into which it can withdraw. It draws the tube about with it held by two hooks on the last abdominal segment.

The larva has a distinct head and a segmented body, three pairs of thoracic legs and tracheal gills on the abdominal segments.

10. Larva of Caddis Fly—*Limnophilus sp.*

Segmented larva, with three pairs of thoracic legs and filamentous tracheal gills. The tube is formed from grains of sand, pieces of moss and sometimes broken snail shells. The outer surface of the case is always rough.

11. Larva of the Alder Fly—*Sialis lutaria F.*

Body in distinct segments, with three pairs of thoracic legs and seven pairs of jointed, filamentous, hairy, tracheal gills. The body ends in a long, pointed, hairy abdominal projection.

The larva lives in the mud, feeding on small animals. Pupation takes place on land in the soil.

12. Dragonfly larva

The larva is in distinct segments; head, thorax and abdomen clearly distinguishable. There are three pairs of thoracic legs and the beginnings of wings.

The main characteristic is the "mask" which is attached below the mouth. At rest the mask is under the head but it can be shot out with great speed. At the end are sharp pincers which seize the prey. The structure of the mask is a factor in separating the different species of dragonfly larvae.

A second characteristic is the presence or absence of the leaf-shaped tracheal gills on the abdomen. They are found in the genera *Lestes*, *Agrion* and *Calopteryx*; but not in the

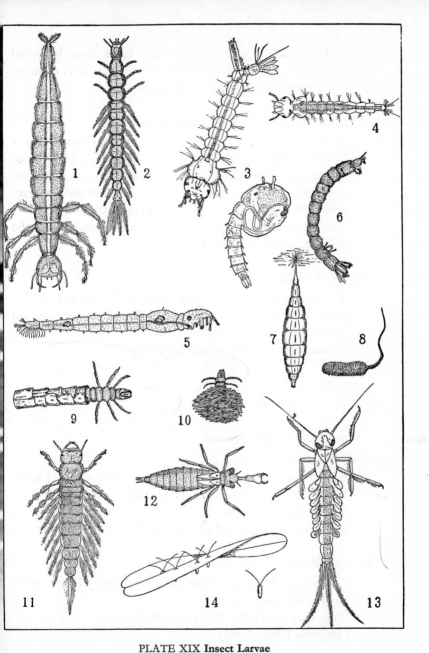

PLATE XIX Insect Larvae

1. Larva of the Great Diving Beetle; 2. Larva of the Whirligig Beetle; 3. Larva and pupa of the Mosquito; 4. Larva of the Malaria Mosquito; 5. Larva of the Phantom Midge; 6. Larva of the Midge; 7. Larva of the Chameleon Fly; 8. Larva of the Drone Fly; 9. 10. Larvae of Caddis Flies; 11. Larva of the Alder Fly; 12. Larva of a Dragonfly; 13. Larva of the Mayfly; 14. Eggs of the Water Stick Insect on a leaf and one natural size.

genera *Libellula* and *Aeschna*. The latter have branched tracheae in the rectum (rectal gills), and water is continuously pumped in and out of the anus.

13. **Larva of the Mayfly**—*Cloeon dipterum L.*

$\pm$ $\frac{1}{2}$ inch long. A transparent, segmented larva with a distinct head, three pairs of thoracic legs, the beginnings of wings and seven pairs of plate-like, double tracheal gills on the abdominal segments. The last segment has three characteristic hairy "tails". Found in stagnant water.

The shape of the tracheal gills can be used to separate the different species of Mayfly larvae.

14. **Eggs of the Water Stick Insect**—*Ranatra linearis L.*

This is an example of a water insect which lays eggs which are easy to see. They have two threads (breathing tubes) which are protruded through a leaf on the surface of the water. Air is thus able to reach the eggs.

ADULT ANIMALS

(i) BEETLES *(Coleoptera)*

1. *Haliplus flavicollis Sturm.*

Body ovoid, wing covers striped, but not spotted. $\frac{1}{8}$ inch. Lives among water plants in stagnant water. Swims by moving the back legs.

There are 16 species of *Haliplus* in Britain, some common.

2. **Screech Beetle**—*Hygrobia hermanni F.*

Upper side flatter than the underside. Rusty-brown with large black mark. $\frac{1}{2}$ inch.

Found in ponds as far north as Yorkshire.

(Hygrobia tarda Hrbst.)

PLATE XX **Beetles**

1. *Halipus flavicollis*; 2. Screech Beetle; 3. *Hydroporus palustris*; 4. Rusty Water Beetl
5. *Coelambus novemlineatus*; 6. *Agabus sturmi*; 7. *Rantus notatus*; 8. Smoky Diving Beet
9. *Graphoderus cinereus*; 10. *Acilius sulcatus*; 11. *Hydaticus transversalis*; 12. Gr
Diving Beetle; 13. Whirligig Beetle; 14. Silver Water Beetle; 15. Small Black Wa
Beetle; 16. *Hydrobius fuscipes*; 17. Broad-necked Water Beetle; 18. *Spercheus emarginat*
19. *Berosus luridus*; 20. Leaf Beetle; 21. Ground Beetle.

3. *Hydroporus palustris L.*

> Oval, rusty-brown with a darker mark on the head, protho-
> rax and wings covers. $\frac{1}{8}$ inch.
> There are 37 species *of Hydroporus* in Britain.

4. **Rusty Water Beetle**—*Hyphydrus ferrugineus L.*

> Rusty brown, with small black spots, an almost globular
> body. The mesothorax cannot be seen. The claws on the
> back pair of legs are of a different shape.
> Common. $\frac{1}{8}$ inch.

5. *Coelambus novemlineatus Steph.*

> Head yellow with a darker back edging. Prothorax yellow
> with a dark spot in the middle. Wing-covers each have four
> longitudinal, black lines. The mid-line is also black. Belly
> black. Legs brown-yellow.
> Local. $\frac{1}{8}$ inch.

6. *Agabus sturmi Gyll.*

> Black head and brown wings, edged with yellow-brown.
> Underside black.
> In ponds. $\pm$ $\frac{2}{8}$ inch.

7. *Rantus notatus F.*

> Yellow and black; black specks on the wings and three
> narrow, yellow stripes down them.
> Rare. $\pm$ $\frac{1}{2}$ inch.

8. **Smoky Diving Beetle**—*Colymbetes fuscus L.*

> Black head with red flecks. The prothorax has orange-yellow
> bands. Wing-covers dark brown, edges yellow-brown.
> Underparts black. The first two pairs of legs of the male
> have small suckers. $\pm$ $\frac{3}{8}$ inch.

9. *Graphoderus cinereus* L.

Oval, short but quite broad. General colour is light brownish-yellow with black bands on the head and across the neck. The wing-covers have many black speckles and a yellow edge. ♂ has many small suckers on the leg joints.

Rare. ± ⅔ inch.

10. *Acilius sulcatus* L.

Very flat. Yellow and black. ♂ has longitudinal ridges on the wing-covers marked by small, black spots. One large and many very small suckers are on each of the first leg joints. ♀ has four broad, longitudinal grooves on the wing-covers, containing long hairs.

Common in ponds. ± ¾ inch.

11. *Hydaticus transversalis* Pentopp.

Rather solid. Prothorax has the hind edge dark and is greenish black. Wing-covers similar with a yellow edge and cross-bands parallel to the lower edge. Underparts brownish. Legs yellow. ½ inch.

Southern England.

12. **Great Diving Beetle**—*Dytiscus marginalis* L.

Olive-green with yellow bands on the head, prothorax and wing-covers. Underparts and legs yellow. Wing-covers smooth in the ♂, with longitudinal grooves in the ♀. Threadlike feelers.

Common. 1½ inches.

Larva: see page 85.

Dytiscus circumcinctus Ahr.

Underparts brown-yellow, not flecked. Very like no. 12. Wing-covers of ♂ smooth, of the ♀ grooved but not down the whole length.

Rare and local. 1½ inches.

Dytiscus circumflexus F.

Not as broad as the previous one. Rather wide yellow margin. Underparts flecked with olive-green.

Rare and local. 1¼ inches.

Dytiscus latissimus L.

Larger. Almost black with broad yellow margins. Underparts black. Wing-covers smooth in ♂, grooved in ♀.

Very rare. ± 2 inches.

13. **Whirligig Beetle**—*Gyrinus sp.*

(*Gyrinus natator* is the commonest).

Egg-shaped, very solid. Swims on the water. Glistening black with a blue sheen. Legs reddish-yellow.

The upper part of the eye sees above the water, the lower part sees below. ± $\frac{1}{5}$ inch.

Common in stagnant water.

Larva: see page 86.

14. **Silver Water Beetle**—*Hydrous piceus* L.

Black. Broken ridges with fine hairs on the wing-covers. Long swimming hairs round the edge. Feelers club-shaped. To get air the animal pushes one feeler above water and by moving this fresh air becomes trapped under the body. Feeds on plants. ± 1¾ inches.

The female spins a cocoon in which the eggs are laid. This is fastened under a floating leaf and has a funnel by which fresh air is obtained.

Local. Found in southern counties of England.

Larva: see page 85.

15. **Small Black Water Beetle**—*Hydrophilus caraboides* L.

Black, usually with a greenish sheen. Legs red-brown. Five broken ridges on the wing-covers. Spins a cocoon for the eggs.

Local in southern counties. ± ¾ inch.

16. *Hydrobius fuscipes L.*

Very convex, black with brown, metallic sheen. Legs reddish-brown.

Common. ± ½ inch.

17. **Broad-necked Water Beetle**—*Helophorus aquaticus L.*

Only slightly convex. Head and neck metallic green or copper-coloured. Wing-covers brown or brown-yellow, with a metallic sheen and a few, darker flecks on the lower half.

Fairly common. ± ¼ inch.

18. *Spercheus emarginatus Schall.*

Short and broad, very convex. Brown-red or light-coloured with a few, darker flecks along the join of the wing-covers which are slightly grooved. ± ½ inch.

(In the picture the head of the animal is hidden by the body).

Probably not now found in Great Britain.

19. *Berosus luridus L.*

Brown or brown-yellow. Prothorax thickly spotted, dark brown, with a lighter band on each side. Wing-covers dark brown with a line of dots bordering the lighter, lower portion. ± ⅙ inch.

Local. Rare.

20. **Leaf Beetle**—*Donacia crassipes F.*

Small head, prothorax narrower than the rest of the body. Golden-green, with longitudinal, broken markings. Legs brown-yellow. Back legs with distinct spines at the inner angle of the thigh. ± ½ inch.

Often found on the leaves of the White or Yellow Water Lilies. There are several species of *Donacia* known and also some of the related genus *Plateumaris*.

Fairly common.

The eggs are laid on the undersides of floating leaves. They are in a double row near a small hole which the female makes in the leaf.

21. **Ground Beetle**—*Carabus clathratus L.*

Dark, bronze-coloured. On each wing-cover are three copper-coloured grooves and golden speckles.

In boggy places. Rare. $\pm$ 1 inch.

Carabus violaceus is common and is a dark purplish-black.

(ii) MOTHS *(Lepidoptera)*

22. **Drinker Moth**—*Philudoria potatoria L.*

(Cosmotriche potatoria) (Odonestris potatoria)

Ochreous yellow, the ♂ rather more brown. There are two silver-white marks on the front wings and also an oblique, wavy, brown line on each. There is another smaller wavy line nearer the body, also a fainter line on the hind-wing. Common in July and August.

There are two varieties of this moth:— the yellow or yellow-brown and the red-brown or dark brown. The variation is most apparent in the males, the females being more alike. The name 'Drinker' refers to the caterpillars, which live on grassy plants in damp places like the banks of streams.

23. **Powdered Wainscot Moth**—*Simyra albovenosa (Goeze)*

(Arsilonche albovenosa)

Front wings white with a dusting of brown and two long brown lines. Hind wings white. The caterpillar lives on grass.

24. **Five-spotted Burnet**—*Zygaena trifolii Esp.*

Front wings blue-green with red spots. Hind wings red with broad, rather blue-black borders. Found in swampy pastures or on clover.

There are various other species of *Zygaena*, which closely resemble each other.

25. Tiger Moth—*Arctia caia L.*

Front wings coffee-coloured with white criss-crossing bands. Hind wings red with large blue-black spots. The width of the white bands varies greatly. Sometimes they are very wide and in other specimens will be very narrow. The caterpillar is red-brown and has very long hairs. It is often called the "Woolly Bear".
Common.

26. Elephant Hawk Moth—*Deilephila elpenor L.*
(Chaerocampa elpenor)

Front wings olive-green having two broad, oblique, red-violet lines and a red-violet edging. Hind-wings are a light red-violet with black towards the body and along the front edge. The body is sharply pointed.
Common but local.

27. Light Knot Grass Moth—*Apatele menyanthidis View.*
(Acronicta menyanthidis)

Front wings grey, with darker markings and black lines. Back wings light grey. Rare.
Caterpillar found on the Buckbean and Bog Myrtle.

28. Bulrush Wainscot Moth—*Nonagria typhae Thnbg.*

Front wings brown-yellow with white veins and black spots. Back wings yellowish, darker in the middle.
The caterpillar lives in the stalks of the Reed Mace.
Commoner in the south.

Brown-veined Wainscot Moth—*Nonagria neurica Hb.*
Front wings brown with a black bloom and black specks along the sides. Back wings grey with a black dusting.
Rather rare. Caterpillar lives in reed stems.

29. Brown China Mark Moth—*Hydrocampa nymphaeata L.*

Small, with grey wings and an irregular brown pattern.
$\pm$ 1 inch.

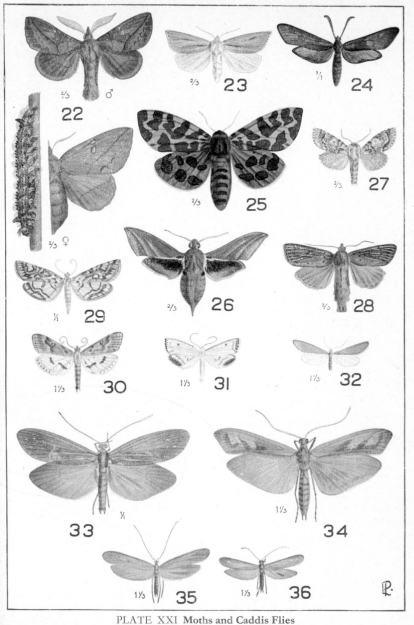

PLATE XXI **Moths and Caddis Flies**
22. Drinker Moth; 23. Powdered Wainscot Moth; 24. Five-spotted Burnet; 25. Tiger Moth;
26. Elephant Hawk Moth; 27. Light Knot Grass Moth; 28. Bulrush Wainscot Moth;
29. Brown China Mark Moth; 30. *Paraponyx stratiotata*; 31. Small China Mark Moth;
32. Water Moth; 33. Large Caddis Fly; 34. Caddis Fly; 35. *Molanna angustata*
36. *Neureclipsis bimaculata*.

The eggs are laid on the leaves of Water Lilies or Pondweeds. The young caterpillars bore their way into the plants. They bite out small pieces of the leaves and spin threads to make them into a covering. This falls to the bottom, where the animal passes the winter. It breathes through its skin. In the spring the case is filled with air and the animal breathes by tracheae. The pupa metamorphoses inside a similar cocoon which is attached to a plant.

(Nymphula nymphaeata)

30. *Paraponyx stratiotata L.*

The light-green caterpillar lives among the leaves of the Water Soldier fastened together with silk. It breathes by tracheal gills. The pupa has a cocoon in the plant and probably breathes air from the air-chambers of the plant. This air can pass into the cocoon and thus to the pupa. The adult has yellow-brown fore-wings and white hind-wings, both with brown spots and markings.

Rare.

31. **Small China Mark Moth**—*Cataclysta lemnata L.*

Along the hind-edge of the back wings runs a velvety-black, yellow-edged band, having four silver-white spots. ¾—1 inch.

The dark green caterpillar builds a covering of leaf-stalks and silk; this is later filled with air and pupation takes place. The moth metamorphoses in one summer. See no. 29.

32. **Water Moth**—*Acentropus niveus Ol.*

Fore-wings light grey with a grey-brown border at the front edge. Hind-wings white. ½—¾ inch.

This unique moth goes under the water to lay its eggs. The caterpillar is olive-green and usually lives on different kinds of Pondweeds, but can also be found on other plants. It probably takes its air from the air-spaces in the plant, into which the young caterpillars bore their way. There they are able to spend the winter. Other larvae make a case from two leaves fastened together with silk. Pupation takes place in a cocoon filled with air. The winged females come out of the water and fly about but there is another kind of female which has only rudimentary wings and which stays in the water. The life-history is not fully known.

(iii) CADDIS FLIES *(Trichoptera)*

33. Large Caddis Fly—*Phryganea grandis L.*

Dorsal side brown, underside grey-brown. The legs have light and dark rings. Fore-wings dark, brown-red marbled with single white flecks. The hind-wings are yellowish with a brown edge.

Larva: see page 88.

34. Caddis Fly—*Limnophilus rhombicus L.*

Front wings ochre-yellow with single white flecks, the centre one being diamond-shaped. Hind-wings rather blue with an ochreous edge.

Larva: see page 88.

35. *Molanna angustata Curt.*

Fore-wings grey-yellow. The antennae are as long as the wings. Wing-span about ¾ inch.

This caddis-fly has a larva which makes a characteristic tube of fine particles of sand and is therefore practically invisible against the sandy bottom. Found in still water.

36. *Neureclipsis bimaculata L.*

Like no. 35 but smaller and the antennae are shorter than the wings.

The larva spins a funnel-shaped web, in which it catches all kinds of small animals sent into it by the water currents.

37. **Demoiselle Fly**—*Calopteryx virgo* L.

(Agrion virgo)

♂ steel-blue or dark metallic green with dark brown, metallic, shining wings. ♀ green-gold with light brownish wings having white speckles at the front edge.

Wing-span 2½ inches.

Larva with tracheal and rectal gills for breathing.

Common locally. Widespread but mostly found in the south.

Banded Demoiselle—*Calopteryx splendens* H.

(Agrion splendens)

♂ with dark brown cross-bar on the wings. ♀ with light greenish wings. Wing-span: 2½ inches.

Larva with tracheal and rectal gills for breathing.

Common in Midlands and the south.

38. **Green Lestes**—*Lestes viridis v. d. Lind.*

(Lestes sponsa)

Body bronze-green. Wings transparent with yellow-brown speckles on the front edge. Held horizontally when at rest. Wing-span $\pm$ 2 inches.

Larva has tracheal gills.

Common locally.

39. **Dragonfly**—*Sympecma fusca v.d.Lind.*

Bronze-green flecks on the thorax and abdomen. Orange flecks on the front edge of the wings. The wings are held backwards when at rest. Wing-span $\pm$ 1 inch.

40. **Four-spotted Libellula**—*Libellula quadrimaculata* L.

Body has a broad abdomen, pointed at the tip and is yellow-brown with a black tip and yellow marks at the sides. Wings transparent, with a blue sheen, 2 darker spots on the front edge of each and black at the bases.

Wing-span 3 inches.

Common locally. Widespread.

41. **Green-spotted Aeschna**—*Aeschna cyanea Müll.*
Body blue, sometimes more or less green. Wings transparent, with a beautiful venation. Wing-span 3 inches.
Common in south of England, rarer in the north.

Brown Aeschna—*Aeschna grandis L.*
Body rusty-brown, wings transparent and yellowish. ♂ with blue, ♀ with yellow flecks on the abdomen.
Common in the south, rare in the north.
Wing-span 4 inches.

42. **Common Ischnura**—*Ischnura elegans v.d.Lind.*
Upperside of body black, abdomen bronze-coloured. Wings clear and glassy with a small black fleck on each. At rest, the wings are lifted up.
Very common. Wing-span ± 1 inch.

43. **Variable Coenagrion**—*Agrion pulchellum v.d.Lind.*
(Coenagrion pulchellum)
Upperside of body black, with blue cross-bands. On the front edges of each wing is a red-brown spot.
Wing-span 1½ inches.
Larva has external tracheal gills.
Common locally.

(v) **TWO-WINGED FLIES** *(Diptera)*

44. **Midge**—*Chironomus plumosus L.*
(Tendipus plumosus)
The feelers of the ♂ consist of 14 joints with long, soft hairs giving a feathery appearance. In the ♀ the feelers are short and less hairy. ± ½ inch.
Larva: see page 87.

45. **Green Midge**—*Glyptotendipus viridis Macq.*
Like no. 44 but smaller and green in colour. In the ♂ the first legs and the tarsae of the other legs have downy hairs. ± ¼ inch. Very rare.

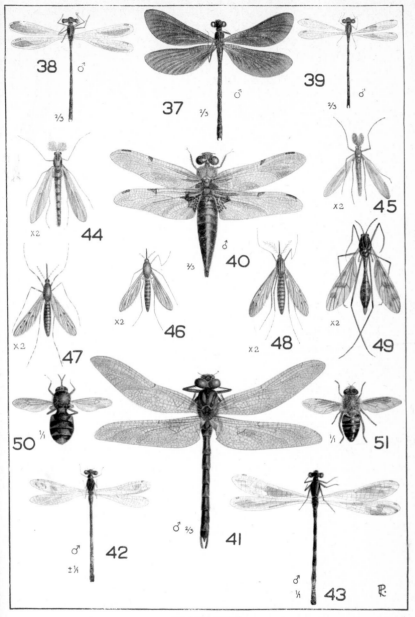

PLATE XXII

37. Demoiselle Fly; 38. Green Lestes; 39. Dragonfly; 40. Four-spotted Libellula; 41. Green-spotted Aeschna; 42. Common Ischnura; 43. Variable Coenagrion; 44. Midge; 45. Green Midge; 46. Gnat or Mosquito; 47. Ringed Mosquito; 48. Malaria Mosquito; 49. Crane-fly; 50. Chameleon Fly; 51. Drone Fly.

46. Gnat or Mosquito—*Culex pipiens L.*
Thorax yellow-brown, abdomen light with dark brown rings. Wings transparent, not spotted. Feelers shorter than the mouthparts. ¼ inch.
Larva on page 86.

47. Ringed Mosquito—*Theobaldia annulata Schr.*
Whole body brown, darker rings on the abdomen. Legs have white rings. Brown spots on the wings. ± ⅜ inch.

48. Malaria Mosquito—*Anopheles maculipennis Meig.*
This mosquito always settles with the body at a distinct angle to the surface. This point affords the best method of identification. The feelers are longer than the mouth-parts. Other wise it is much like no. 47. ± ⅜ inch.
Larva:page 86.

49. Crane-fly or Daddy-long-legs—*Ptychoptera contaminata L.*
(Liriope contaminata)
Body shiny black, with rust-coloured bands and spots on the abdomen. Single brown flecks on the wings. The abdomen is very narrow anteriorly, then it broadens and finally ends in a point.
Found on plants by the water. Body ± ½ inch.

50. Chameleon Fly—*Stratiomys furcata L.*
Antennae arise so close together that they look like the letter Y. Abdomen broader than the thorax, with yellow spots. ± ⅜ inch.
Common on flowers by the water, especially *Umbelliferae*.
Larva on page 87.

51. Drone Fly— *Eristalomyia tenax L.*
(Eristalis tenax)
A glider; often wrongly named, as it rather resembles a

honey-bee. It can be distinguished from this as it has only one pair of wings. Seen in the autumn. $\pm$ ⅜ inch.
Larva: see page 87.

(vi) LACE WINGS *(Neuroptera)*

52. **Alder Fly**—*Sialis flavilatera L.*

(Sialis lutaria).
Body brown-black. Wings thickly veined, rather brownish. Flies badly. $\pm$ ⅜ inch.
Common on plants on the banks.
Larva: see page 88.

(vii) WATER BUGS *(Hemiptera)*

53. *Salda saltatoria L.*

Lives on the bank. Body is ovate, yellow with black spots, with a characteristic head. ⅛ inch. Has characteristic mouthparts, including a beak. Feeds on small animals which it catches with the first pair of legs. Common.
The larva shows incomplete metamorphosis.

54. **Water Boatman**—*Notonecta glauca L.*

Swims on its back, a useful characteristic for identification. The last pair of legs function as swimming legs and have 2 rows of swimming hairs. The dorsal side may be variously coloured. The first part, with the head, is greenish; the mesothorax darker; the wings brown, sometimes with dark brown or blue marks. The underside is very dark. Under water the belly appears silvery and glistening, owing to the air which is entangled in the hairs. There is also an air-bubble caught under the abdomen. ⅜ inch.

55. **Water Bug**—*Plea atomaria Pallas*

Short, rather broad. About $\frac{1}{10}$ inch across.

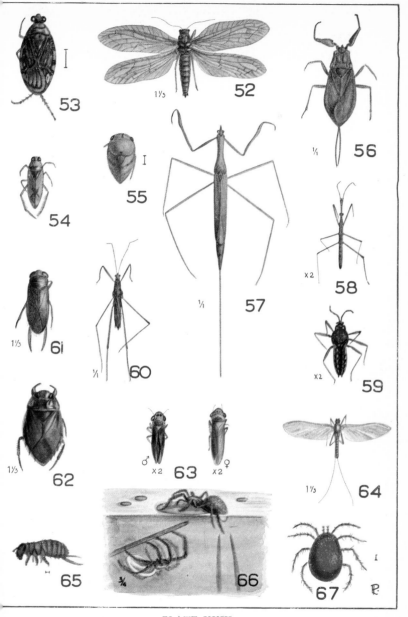

PLATE XXIII

52. Alder Fly; 53. *Salda saltatoria*; 54. Water Boatman; 55. Water Bug; 56. Water Scorpion; 57. Water Stick Insect; 58. Water Measurer; 59. Water Cricket; 60. Pond Skater; 61. Lesser Water Boatman; 62. Water Bug; 63. *Tettigoniella viridis*; 64. Mayfly; 65. Water Bristle-tail; 66. Water Spider; 67. Water Mite.

56. **Water Scorpion**—*Nepa cinerea L.*

(Nepa rubra L.)

The front legs have developed to catch prey. On the abdomen there is a long breathing tube by which the animal hangs from the water surface. By means of this tube air is passed under the wings, so that the animal can remain under the water.

Common.

57. **Water Stick Insect**—*Ranatra linearis L.*

Like the Water Scorpion, this insect has pincer legs and a long breathing tube. It lives mostly on the bottom and is less common. $1\frac{1}{2}$ inches long.

See page 90.

58. **Water Measurer**—*Hydrometra stagnorum L.*

(Limnobates stagnorum)

Moves about on the water surface. The body is linear. All the legs are of the same length. No wings. $\frac{1}{2}$ inch.

59. **Water Cricket**—*Velia capria Tam.*

The first thoracic segment is as long as it is broad. The other two thoracic segments are very small. The abdomen has 2 distinct lines of orange-yellow marks. No wings. The front legs catch prey; the others are walking legs, by means of which the animal 'rows' itself through the water.

$\pm \frac{3}{8}$ inch.

60. **Pond Skater**—*Gerris rufoscutellatus Latr.*

Moves on the water like no. 59. The first thoracic segment is longer than it is broad. Rust-brown. $\frac{3}{8}$ inch.

Gerris thoracicus Schumm.

Has wings. Dark grey-brown, sides rust-yellow and underside white with silky hairs. $\frac{3}{8}$ inch.

61. **Lesser Water Boatman**—*Corixa punctata Ill.*

Shiny greenish-brown with smooth, black marbled wing-covers. Underside brown-yellow. The first thoracic segment is very broad and covers the mesothorax. ½ inch.
Common.

62. **Water Bug**—*Ilyocoris cimicoides L.*

Brown, ovate, with a broad head. The front legs are used as pincers for the animal to seize its prey. ½ inch.
Common in still or slowly moving water.
(Naucoris cimicoides L.)

(viii) GRASSHOPPERS *(Orthoptera)*

63. *Tettigoniella viridis (L.)*
(Cicadella viridis)

The front wings do not overlap. Body yellow. Wings ♂ blue-black; ♀ grass-green, with a yellow edge. ♂ ¼ inch.
♀ ⅜ inch.
Common in the grass on the bank.

(ix) MAYFLIES *(Ephemeroptera)*

64. **Mayfly**—*Cloeon dipterum L.*

Yellow-brown with only 2 transparent wings and 2 white, black-ringed tail filaments. Wings ♀ have a light brown band on the front edge.
Larva: see page 90.

(x) BRISTLE-TAILS *(Thysanura)*

65. **Water Bristle-tail**—*Podura aquatica L.*

Pale blue-black. No wings. A spring-tail on the abdomen. Lives in groups at the edge of ponds, streams etc. Often springs on to the surface. $\pm \frac{1}{25}$ inch.

SPIDERS and MITES *(Arachnida)*

66. **Water Spider**—*Argyroneta aquatica Walck.*

This spider is unique, as it lives *under* the water. It makes a bell-shaped web which is filled with air. The air is carried down entangled in the hairs of the abdomen and the hind-legs, consequently the animal appears a glistening silver when under the water and covered with air bubbles. The eggs are laid under the diving-bell and later the young spiders live there until they can carry air bubbles for themselves.

67. Water Mite—*Hydrarachna sp.*

The picture shows a red water mite about $\frac{1}{25}$ inch in size. The body is unsegmented and bears 4 pairs of legs. There are many species of this animal, some up to $\frac{1}{8}$ inch in size, and they are of many different colours. It is difficult to distinguish them. The larva lives as a temporary parasite on bugs and beetles. The larvae bury their mouth-parts into the soft skin of the prey as soon as they are hatched and change to tiny, red bubbles.

FISH *(Pisces)*

Everyone will be familiar with the general appearance of a fish. The body is adapted for movement in the water and is usually streamlined to facilitate this. Head and trunk merge into each other, without any neck or shoulders. The movement of the body is largely brought about by the strong, muscular tail, which has a large fin. The other fins have the functions of maintaining balance and helping the intake of water for respiration.

The following fins can be distinguished: a dorsal fin, which is sometimes in two or three parts; a tail fin; a pair of pectoral fins, close to the gill-covers; a pair of pelvic fins, sometimes very far back and sometimes far forward, and lastly a ventral fin, close behind the anus (the opening of the intestine) and thus close to the tail. The fins are supported by fin-rays. These are usually very soft but sometimes they are hard and pointed, so that they can inflict wounds. The skeleton of the fish may be entirely of bone or may be made of cartilage (e.g. in the Sturgeon).

All fish breathe by gills. In the bony fishes and also in the Sturgeon, these are covered by a gill-cover so that the gill-slits cannot be seen. In the living fish the gill-covers are continuously opening and closing, thus enabling the water to escape. In the rest of the cartilaginous fish there are no gill-covers and a number of gill-slits can be seen along the sides of the body. In the Lampreys, for example, there are small round gill-openings.

Fish usually have scales which overlap like tiles. Over the scales is the epidermis, often slimy, so that the living fish is difficult to hold in one's hand.

The back of a fish is usually dark and the belly light-coloured. Consequently, if the fish is looked at from above it will not show up against the bottom, and it is not easily seen in the water from below or from the side; thus it is protected from its enemies. This protective coloration is even more apparent in the flat-fish, e.g. the Flounder, which live on the bottom, lying not on the belly but on the side of the body. During the development of the young animal the body is at first normally fish-like, then the head twists so that both eyes come to lie on the same side. The side which is thus uppermost becomes the same colour as the bottom of the pond or stream, while the underside usually remains white.

Most fish have a specialised sense organ known as the lateral line. This line is usually formed by a row of perforated scales. The tiny openings lead to a fine tube which runs under the scales from the head to the tail. In this tube are many nerve endings. It is probable that this organ is used to detect movements and changes of pressure in the water and so sense what is ahead.

Reproduction takes place from the large numbers of eggs which are laid. In most cases these are left to their fate, but some species provide them with care and protection. One example of this is the Stickleback, which makes a spherical nest guarded by the male.

Most fish feed on small animals on the water surface or on submerged plants and animals, i.e. protozoans, small crustaceans etc. and also on the eggs of fish and other animals and on young fish. The carnivorous fish eat small fish, tadpoles, young birds etc. These fish have large teeth, while the plankton-eaters have only small teeth or none at all.

1. **Perch**—*Perca fluviatilis L.*

Back green with 5-7 darker cross-bars; underside yellowish. On the hinder part of the spiked dorsal fin is a black fleck. The soft dorsal fin has 14 fin-rays.

A carnivorous fish, feeding in still, fresh water. 8-16 inches.

2. **River Pike**—*Stizostedium lucioperca (L.)*

Back dark green-grey, with flecks and indistinct cross-bars; underparts almost white. The first dorsal fin has 14 hard fin-rays, the second has about 20.

Carnivorous. In large lakes, canals and rivers.

Not in Great Britain. 16-32 inches.

3. **Pope or Ruffe**—*Acerina cernua (L.)*

Brownish-olive with dark flecks on the body and fins, underparts silver-white. Only 1 dorsal fin but the first part has spikes and the hinder part is soft. The eyes are placed obliquely in the head.

Carnivorous. In fresh water. Rather scarce.

Absent from Scotland and Ireland. 6-8 inches.

4. **Bullhead or Miller's Thumb**—*Cottus gobio L.*

Brown-green with dark, irregular spots. The first dorsal fin is spiked and is shorter than the second. Large pectoral fins. There is a pointed spine on the gill-cover. The eggs are laid in a hole on the bottom of the stream. ♂ guards the nest.

Lives in moving fresh water. 4-6 inches.

5. **Three-spined Stickleback**—*Gasterosteus aculeatus L.*

The first dorsal fin consists of 3 separate spines. Back greenish, underparts silver-white. In the spring the ♂ has the back blue-green and the underparts bright red.

Very common in streams and ponds, found in fresh and

brackish water and even in the sea. 2-4 inches.

It is known in various forms, distinguished by the number and position of the large scales; in fresh water is *var. leiurus*; in the sea is *var. trachurus*.

The male stickleback makes a spherical nest of water weeds. The female lays the eggs in it, after which she is driven away and the male puts the seminal fluid over them. Usually the male fertilizes eggs laid by several different females. The male guards the nest, which is partially under the sand and, by moving his fins, introduces fresh water over the 32-70 eggs. For a short time the young fish are also guarded by the male.

6. **Ten-spined Stickleback**—*Pungitius pungitius L.*

The first dorsal fin consists of 9-11 spines. Very dark grey. Back black.

Common in fresh water. Fastens the nest on to plants. Breeding habits like no. 5. 1½—3 inches.

(Pygosteus pungitius)

7. **Burbot**—*Lota lota (L.)*

Brown-green, dark marbling, the dorsal fin roundish. The second dorsal fin has 20—70 fin-rays and reaches to the level of the anus. Pelvic fins in front of the pectoral fins. On the under-lip is a long, thread-like feeler, and there are two small feelers on the front of the nostrils.

Carnivorous. In fresh water. Local, mostly found in rivers near the east coast. 1-2 feet.

8. **Flounder**—*Pleuronectes flesus L.*

Flat fish. Upperside brown-green with pale yellow flecks. Along the lateral line and the bases of the fins are rough tubercules.

Common in river-mouths, travels up the rivers and is sometimes found in inland waters. 8-20 inches.

(Platichthys flesus)

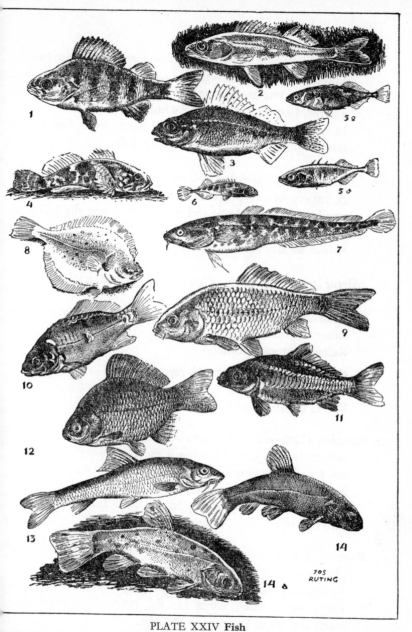

PLATE XXIV **Fish**

1. Perch; 2. River Pike; 3. Pope or Ruffe; 4. Bullhead; 5. Three-spined Stickleback; 6.
Ten-spined Stickleback; 7. Burbot; 8. Flounder; 9. Common Carp; 10. Leather Carp;
11. Mirrot or King Carp; 12. Crucian Carp; 13. Barbel; 14. Tench; 14a. Golden Tench.

9. **Common Carp**—*Cyprinus carpio* L.

Back dark, bronze-coloured; underparts yellow-brown. Long, dark, dorsal fin with 3-4 hard and 17-22 soft fin-rays. The other fins are red or yellowish. On the upper-lip are 4 barbs. Large scales over the whole body.

In rivers and lakes. Often kept in stock-pools. Introduced into England in the 17th. century. 1-2 feet.

10. **Leather Carp**—*Cyprinus carpio var. nudus (Bl.)*

A variety of the previous species. The scales are mostly smaller, along the back and the tail are some single, large, flat scales.

Raised in stock-pools. Rare.

11. **Mirror or King Carp**—*Cyprinus carpio var. rex cyprinorum Kramer*

Another variety of no. 9. The large flat scales can be seen along the back and along the sides of the lateral line.

Raised in stock-pools.

Gold Carp—*Cyprinus carpio var. auratus*

Gold-coloured, back with darker flecks.

Found in ornamental ponds. 8-20 inches.

12. **Crucian Carp**—*Carassius carassius (L.)*

Differs from no. 9 in having a more compact and higher body and in having no barbs. In the dorsal fin are 3 or 4 hard and 16-19 soft fin-rays.

In lakes and rivers, mostly in the east. Introduced. 6-16 inches.

13. **Barbel**—*Barbus barbus (L.)*

Light greenish-brown with red fins, except for the short, dark-grey, dorsal fin which has 3 hard and 8-9 soft fin-rays. There are 4 thick barbs on the protruding upper-lip. Scales not large. Lateral line straight.

In fresh and sometimes in brackish water.
Local, found in the Thames and the Trent. 12-20 inches.

14. **Tench**—*Tinca tinca (L.)*
Brown-green with a golden sheen. Very small scales, sunk down in the skin. Body compressed sideways, bearing roundish, dark fins. Two small barbs.
Found in still water. 8-16 inches.

14a. **Golden Tench**—*Tinca tinca var. aurata (Bl.)*
Golden-yellow with small dark flecks and white fins.
Found in ornamental pools. 8-16 inches.

15. **Gudgeon**—*Gobio gobio (L.)*
Bluish on the back and sides, underparts yellowish-white. Dorsal and tail fins brown streaked. Body almost cylindrical. Large scales. Two distinct barbs.
In fresh and brackish water, especially in rivers. 4-8 inches.

16. **Minnow**—*Phoxinus phoxinus (L.)*
Back olive-green, black marbling, with a gold-coloured stripe on each side. Underside light. Body almost cylindrical. Lateral line is only visible for a short distance. No barbs. Anal fin is further back than the dorsal fin.
In the mating season the females are red with a metallic sheen.
Common in running streams. $2\frac{3}{4}$-$3\frac{3}{4}$ inches.

17. **Bitterling**—*Rhodeus amarus (Bl.)*
Silver-blue and shiny. In the mating season red-coloured with blue metallic sheen, especially in the ♂. Lateral line short. Dark blue or green stripe from the middle of the tail to the middle of the body. The ♀ develops a long ovipositor in the breeding season.
Not found in Great Britain. $2\frac{1}{2}$-4 inches.

18. **Bleak**—*Alburnus alburnus (L.)*

A shiny, mother-of-pearl-coloured, long-bodied fish, with a long anal fin. Lateral line curved downwards.

In fresh water, mostly in rivers. Only found in England and mostly in the south and east. 4-8 inches.

19. **White or Silver Bream**—*Blicca bjoerkna (L.)*

Silvery and shiny with darker back and grey fins, the bases being red. Short head with large eyes. Lateral line slightly curved. Long anal fin with 3 hard and 19-23 soft fin-rays. Differs from Common Bream in having bigger scales.

Rather rare and local. 8-12 inches.

20. **Common Bream**—*Abramis brama (L.)*

Shining silver with darker, humped back and brown-grey fins (not red at the base). Small head with small eyes. Lateral line curved. Long anal fin with 3 hard and 23-28 soft fin-rays. Differs from Silver Bream in having smaller scales.

Common in shoals in the south of England and Ireland. 16-30 inches.

21. *Chondrostoma nasus (L.)*

Shining silver with dark blue back. Long body. Dorsal fin black, other fins reddish. The upper-lip pointed with a short snout beyond the mouth. Lips sharp-edged and horny. 10-20 inches.

Not found in Great Britain.

22. **Rudd**—*Scardinius erythrophthalmus (L.)*

Brown-green with a silvery shine. Red fins and a golden-brown glow over the scales. Red fleck by the eyes. A slanting, upturned snout. Lateral line slightly curved

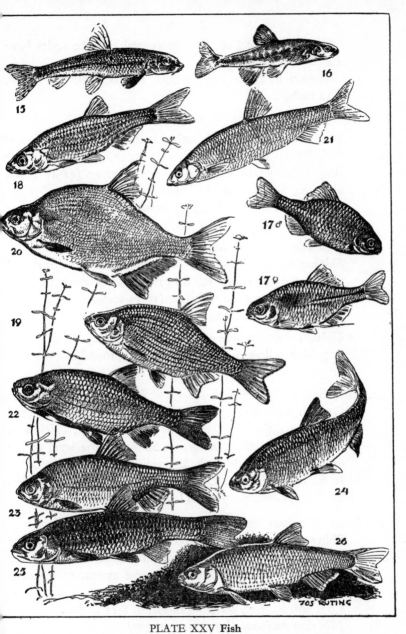

PLATE XXV **Fish**

15. Gudgeon; 16. Minnow; 17. Bitterling; 18. Bleak; 19. White or Silver Bream; 20.
Common Bream; 21. *Chondrostoma nasus*; 22. Rudd; 23. Roach; 24. Orfe or Ide; 25. Chubb;
26. Dace.

(39-42 scales along it). On the ventral side the scales have a sharp keel.

Common in fresh and brackish waters. Rare in Ireland. 8-12 inches.

23. **Roach**—*Rutilus rutilus (L.)*

Blue-green on the back, other parts white with pale red fins. Round the eye there is a green or, sometimes, a red ring. Lateral line with a downwards curve (42-45 scales along it). Scales on the belly have no keel.

Common in fresh water. 6-10 inches.

(Leuciscus rutilus)

24. **Orfe or Ide**—*Leuciscus idus (L.)*

Shining silver with darker back. Fins pale red but dorsal fin and the end of the tail fin grey. Lateral line with slight wavy curves, not very distinct (56-59 scales along it).

In moving water. 12-20 (or 30) inches.

Golden Orfe—*Leuciscus idus var. auratus (L.)*

A golden-yellow or orange-red variety, found in ornamental ponds.

25. **Chubb**—*Squalius cephalus*

Greyish with dark green back and light belly. Pelvic and anal fins red tinged, pectoral fins orange-yellow. Thick head with large mouth opening, extending to the level of the eyes. 44-46 scales along the lateral line.

In fresh, moving water. Local, only in England and Wales. 1-2 feet. *(Leuciscus cephalus (L.))*

26. **Dace**—*Leuciscus leuciscus (L.)*

Shiny white with dark green back. Lateral line rather curved downwards. Mouth opening extends back to the eye. The upper-lip protrudes to some extent. 50-55 scales along the lateral line.

Common in fresh water in England. 8-12 inches.

(Squalius leuciscus) (Leuciscus grislagine)

27. **Pond Loach**—*Misgurnus fossilis (L.)*

Cylindrical body, brown-grey with light, black-stippled stripes along the back and sides. Small mouth opening. Six barbs on the upper-lip and four on the under-lip. 5-10 inches.

Not found in Great Britain.

28. **Stone Loach**—*Nemacheilus barbatulus (L.)*

Cylindrical, yellow-brown body with dark flecks. Cross lines of flecks on the dorsal and tail fins. There are 6 long barbs on the upper-lip.

In clear streams and rivers. 4-6 inches.

(Cobitis barbatula (L.))

29. **Spined Loach**—*Cobitis taenia L.*

The sides of the strong, compressed body have rectangular markings. There are six barbs on the upper-lip and a spine by each eye, which can be erected. On the base of the tail fin is a black stripe.

In fresh water with a muddy bottom. Rare and local. 3¼-4 inches.

30. **Smelt or Sparling**—*Osmerus eperlanus (L.)*

Narrow body. Back blue-green; belly yellowish-white covered with small black flecks. Behind the dorsal fin is a small fat-fin. Large scales. The lateral line runs only as far as the pectoral fin.

A sea fish but also found in brackish water and even in fresh water, especially in river mouths. 3¼-12 inches.

31. **Common River Trout**—*Salmo fario L.*

Back olive-green, shading to a yellowy-green belly with red, sometimes darker, flecks surrounded by a white or blue ring. Behind the dorsal fin is a small fat-fin. Small scales.

In swift-moving, clear streams. 8-16 inches.

Salmon—*Salmo salar* L.

Long, torpedo-shaped body. Back a dark, metallic blue. Belly silver-white. Tail-fin forked. In the male the mouth only opens on one side.

Travels from the sea up the rivers and high into the hills where it spawns, the young fish goes to the sea in the mid-spring and later travels back up the same river. Known in mountain rivers, particularly in Scotland.

Trout—*Salmo trutta* L.

Many varieties of colour, mostly green and orange. Spots are scattered over the body giving a dappled appearance. Tail broad and fleshy, slightly forked, scales more numerous than on the Salmon.

Found in clear lakes and streams over most of the British Isles.

Grayling—*Thymallus thymallus* L.

Long, dorsal fin with 18-24 fin-rays; this distinguishes it from other members of the Salmon family.

Common in England and Wales and south Scotland in clear, fast moving streams with stony bottoms.

32. **Catfish**—*Silurus glanis* L.

Large, flat head. Hind part of the round body and tail are flattened. Large split-shaped mouth with two large barbs on the upper-lip and four smaller ones on the under-lip. Small dorsal fin without a spine. Very long anal fin.

Not in Great Britain. 3½-10½ feet.

33. **Pike**— *Esox lucius* L.

Long, cylindrical fish, green with darker bands. Flat, pointed snout with sharp teeth. The dorsal fin is far back and has no spines.

Carnivorous fish in standing fresh and brackish water, in weedy streams and lakes. Common. 16-40 inches

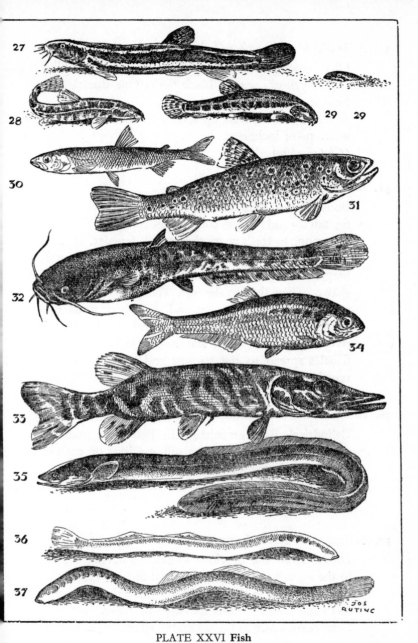

PLATE XXVI **Fish**
27. Pond Loach; 28. Stone Loach; 29. Spined Loach; 30. Smelt; 31. Common River Trout; 32. Catfish; 33. Pike; 34. Allis Shad; 35. Eel; 36. Brook Lamprey; 37. Lampern or River Lamprey.

34. **Allis Shad**—*Alosa alosa (L.)*

Olive-green back and shining silver belly. Gill-covers orange-yellow, with a black fleck. One dorsal fin and a long anal fin. Tail fin with scales.

A sea fish but travels up rivers. Local. Commoner in the west. 16-24 inches.

(Clupea alosa)

35. **Eel**—*Anguilla anguilla (L.)*

Body almost cylindrical, somewhat compressed. Dorsal fin, tail fin and anal fin continuous. No pelvic fins.

Common. In fresh water they are all females. 16-40 inches Eventually the eels travel to the Atlantic Ocean to the Sargasso Sea near South America. Here the eels pair and spawn. Then the females die. The young fish set out for home in the Gulf Stream and take three years to reach England. The little eels (about $\frac{1}{25}$ inch long) travel up the rivers again. The males stay mostly in the estuaries. The females spread to the streams and ponds inland and can travel overland.

36. **Brook or Planer's Lamprey**—*Lampetra planeri (Bloch.)*

Cylindrical. Back greenish, belly lighter. A round mouth opening with blunt teeth. 7 gill-openings on each side. 2 dorsal fins closely following each other. No scales.

Carnivorous fish in moving fresh water. Found in brooks, streams and ditches. 6 inches.

37. **Lampern or River Lamprey**—*Lampetra fluviatilis (L.)*

Differs from the previous species in having sharp teeth in the mouth and 2 separate dorsal fins, of which the back one is larger than the first. At spawning the fish have blunt teeth and the dorsal fins are closer together.

Carnivorous fish, in the sea and in rivers. 12-20 inches.

Sea Lamprey—*Petromyzon marinus* L.

Back olive coloured or grey, marbled with a darker colour. Belly dirty-white. The first dorsal fin is small and starts behind the centre of the body, the second dorsal fin is longer than the first and separated from it by a short space. A sea fish but often found in inland waters. 30-40 inches.

AMPHIBIANS and REPTILES *(Amphibia and Reptilia)*

These two classes of vertebrate animals, which are similar in a number of ways, are here considered together.

The amphibians include the frogs and newts, which have larvae living only in water, though the adult animals, except some newts, live both on land and in the water. The animals are enabled to live on land by having lungs to breathe air; in the water they take in oxygen through the naked skin and also come to the surface to breathe in air.

In the early spring the female frogs are seen to lay large numbers of eggs, each covered by a layer of gelatinous material which swells up on contact with water (frog-spawn) (fig. a). See Plate XXVIII. From these eggs develop small larvae, each having a long tail, external gills and two suckers near the mouth (figs. b_1 and b_2). In the mouth are small, saw-like teeth. Later the external gills are replaced by internal gills (fig. c), and at the same time the legs develop. On the side of the head a small gill-opening appears, which is the outlet for the water which has passed over the gills.

The back legs develop directly, the front legs develop under the gill-cover. In the body there is visible a distinct, spirally-formed intestine. The tail gradually shortens and the front legs break through the gill-opening. The larva has now become a small frog, having lungs to breathe, a definite head but still a stumpy tail which gradually disappears. The metamorphosis takes only a short time but occasionally a tadpole passes the winter in the mud.

The young larvae of different kinds of frogs and toads are

difficult to distinguish from each other. The larval characteristics which are described, refer to the tadpole when the back legs have developed.

The newts develop in a similar way. The eggs are laid separately or in strings attached to water plants and the young larvae develop front legs first and hind legs later.

The reptiles include the crocodiles, snakes, lizards and tortoises. The first and last groups are not found in this country but in or near water are found certain snakes and lizards.

These animals also lay eggs, those of the snakes and lizards having leathery shells, and those of the tortoises chalky shells. The eggs are laid on the land in a hole or a pile of rotten vegation, sometimes they are retained within the body and the young are born alive (oviviviparous). The young animals do not show metamorphosis.

In prehistoric times very large reptiles existed which are known to us through the fossil remains which have been found, particularly in chalky rocks.

AMPHIBIOUS ANIMALS

1. **Smooth Newt**—*Trituris vulgaris L.*

    Brown-grey and green with many black flecks. Five long, black stripes on the head, the outside ones crossing the eyes. In the breeding season the ♂ has a broad crest along back and tail (see picture). During the breeding season the animal lives in water, otherwise on land.

    Common. The only newt found in Ireland. 3-4½ inches.

    In the larva (Ia) the distance between the nostrils is greater than the diameter of the eye but less than the distance from the nostril to the eye. *(Triton vulgaris)*

2. **Crested or Warty Newt**—*Trituris cristatus Laur.*

    Back brown-green with black spots. Belly rust-coloured or orange, also with black spots. ♂ in the breeding season, has

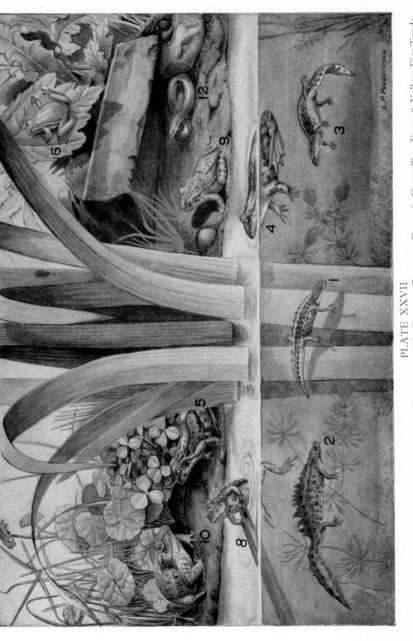

L. P. Pougeroyen

PLATE XXVII

1. Smooth Newt; 2. Crested Newt; 3. Alpine Newt; 4. Edible Frog; 5. Common Frog; 6. Green Tree Frog; 8. Yellow Fire Toad;
9. Midwife Toad; 10. Common Toad; 12. Slow-worm.

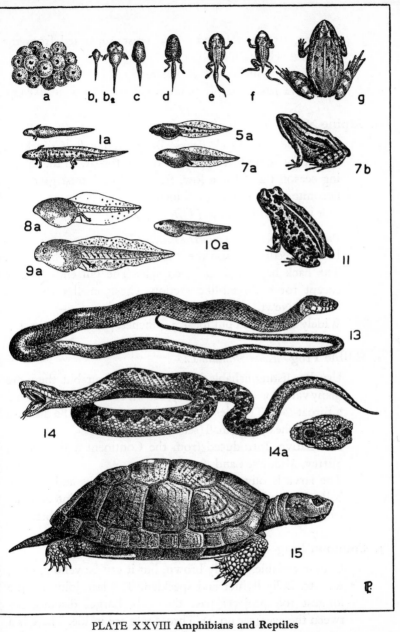

PLATE XXVIII **Amphibians and Reptiles**

a to g. Stages in the life of the Edible Frog; 1a. Larvae of the Smooth Newt; 5a. Larva of
the Common Frog; 7a. Larva of Heath Frog; 7b. Heath Frog; 8a. Larva of Yellow Fire
Toad; 9a. Larva of Midwife Toad; 10a. Larva of Common Toad; 11. Garlic Toad; 13. Grass
Snake; 14. Adder or Viper; 15. European Pond Tortoise.

a large, strong, toothed dorsal crest, separated from the tail crest. Habits like no. 1.

Common. 7¼ inches. *(Triton cristatus)*

The larva has a sharply pointed tail with a thread-like tip.

3. **Alpine Newt**—*Trituris alpestris Laur.*

Back blue with black flecks. Belly orange, not speckled, except for some black speckles on the throat. In the breeding season the ♂ has a low, fringed dorsal crest gradually becoming the tail-crest. 4-6 inches.

Not in the British Isles. *(Triton alpestris)*

Palmated Newt—*Trituris helveticus L.*

In the breeding season the ♂ has black, webbed, hind feet. The back has ridges on each side. The tail ends bluntly except for a thread-like section. Crest smaller than the Smooth Newt.

Widely distributed but local. 3-4 inches. *(Triton helveticus)*

4. **Edible Frog**—*Rana esculenta L.*

Usually distinguishable by the green colour but there are many variations; it may be grey, brown or almost black. ♂ has 2 throat-sacs. The toes are within the webs and the distance between the eyes is small (see no. 5).

Not native. Introduced from the Continent and exists in Surrey, Middlesex and Kent. 4 inches.

The larva is olive-coloured with shiny flecks and a white belly. Tail twice as long as the body, sharply pointed. Total length 3 inches. Metamorphoses in August-September.

5. **Common Frog**—*Rana temporaria L.*

Colour variable, usually brown, but it can be yellow, grey, red etc. Belly lighter and speckled. The last joint of the longest toe projects past the web. Larger distance between the eyes (see no. 4). Throat-sacs are inside. There is a soft, blunt knob on the inner side of the foot behind the small toe, sometimes there is a very small knob on the outside.

Often lives on land. Winters in the mud. Very common. 3¾ inches.

Larva (fig. 5a) dark brown with shiny stipples. Tail 1½-2 × as long as the body, with a blunt tip. Total length 2 inches. Metamorphoses in May-June.

Marsh Frog—*Rana ridibunda L.*

Larger than the Edible Frog. Longer hind legs and a blunted snout. Throat-sacs of ♂ blackish. Back green with black spots.

Introduced from Europe. Now established in Romney Marshes. 4-5½ inches.

6. **Green Tree Frog**—*Hyla arborea L.*

Smooth, shiny head. Back grass-green, sometimes yellow, brown or black. Grey or dark brown band on the back. Belly yellowish. To 2 inches.

Not in Great Britain.

7. **Heath Frog**—*Rana arvalis L.*

Like no. 5 with a pointed snout and no speckles on the back. To 3 inches.

Not in Great Britain.

8. **Yellow Fire Toad**—*Bombinator pachypus Fitz.*

Belly yellow or orange with grey or black marbling. Back olive coloured. To 2 inches.

Not in Great Britain.

9. **Midwife Toad**—*Alytes obstetricans Laur.*

Grey or brownish with black speckles and green or reddish flecks. No throat-sacs. Male carries eggs entangled round his legs. To 2 inches.

Not in Great Britain.

10. **Common Toad**—*Bufo vulgaris Laur*.

Brownish sometimes with darker flecks. Has strong warty skin. Poison glands on the head usually with a dark outer edge. ♀ larger than the ♂. A land animal, laying its eggs in water. Very common. ♀ to 5½ inches. ♂ to 3 inches. Larva (10a) brown-black. Tail 1½× the body length, with a rounded tip. Total length about 1¼ inches.
Metamorphoses in June-July. *(Bufo bufo)*

Natterjack Toad—*Bufo calamita Laur*.
Upper parts grey-green or green and brown speckled. A yellow stripe over the head and back. Short back legs.
Local in England and Wales. To 3 inches.

11. **Garlic Toad**—*Pelobates fuscus Laur*.

Grey or light brown with dark spots and sometimes red dots. No throat-sacs. To 3 inches.
Not in Great Britain.

REPTILES

12. **Slow-worm**—*Anguis fragilis L.*

A legless lizard, often mistaken for a snake. Body cylindrical, somewhat pearly sheen, brown-grey with a dark band along the back and often dark stripes along the sides. Tail as long as the trunk, if picked up by it the tail will come off. Spends the day under stones or moss.
Common, usually on dry ground, particularly in coastal areas. To 20 inches.
In the summer the ♀ gives birth to 8-12 living young. The animal is not dangerous. It feeds on worms, slugs and insects.

13. **Grass Snake**—*Tropidonotus natrix L.*

Back blue-grey or brown with two to six long rows of black spots. On each side behind the head is a yellow-white, black-bordered crossband, together forming a ring. 28-32 inches.

Widely distributed in England and Wales, rare north of Yorkshire. Lays eggs in July in patches of rotting vegetation, under moss or in manure heaps. In August or September the young hatch out. This snake is not dangerous. It can swim. *(Natrix natrix Lac.)*

14. Adder or Viper—*Vipera berus (Merr.)*

Back grey (♂) or brown (♀) with dark flecks on the triangular head and along the well-known zig-zag stripe on the back. Belly dark with light flecks. (Black specimens are also known).

Lives on heaths. Common locally. Venomous. 20-30 inches. The eggs remain in the body and the young are born alive. It is a nocturnal animal. The bite can be dangerous and even fatal. The wound should be cauterized and receive medical attention.

Smooth Snake—*Coronella austriaca Laur.*

Superficially like the Adder. Has a browner colour and smooth, shiny scales. The back markings are different. A more slender body.

Local. Young born alive in August. 20-24 inches.

15. European Pond Tortoise—*Emys orbicularis L.*

Brown or green-black with yellow flecks and stripes. Not very convex. The head can be withdrawn under the shell. Lives in water. Hibernates in the mud. Feeds on small fish. Found on the Continent. To 8 inches.

Not in Great Britain.

BIRDS *(Aves)*

There is no new advice that can be given here on how to distinguish one bird from another: head, neck, rump, wings, legs and tail; all these play a part in distinguishing a bird. The best thing for the observer to do is to get the general impression of the bird and sometimes this is sufficient for identification. Quiet observation allows one to observe the bird's behaviour and find out much more about it than its name.

In the descriptions that follow, the most obvious colours and shapes have been given, with other particulars necessary to name the bird.

The wing, really the bird's arm, has large and small primary feathers. These give strength and, next to the shaft, a broad and a small portion can be seen. The small primaries are attached to a large fore-arm bone, the large ones to two reduced fingers. The thumb bears a small wing. The small primaries are often strikingly coloured; for example, at the ends, forming the wing-mirrors. The large primaries form both the top and the tip of the wing. The front edge of the wing and the primaries are, to some extent, covered by smaller feathers.

To save space in the short descriptions that follow, the following abbreviations have been used:-

S	spends the summer here but does not always breed here.
W	winter visitor.
R	resident and remains all the year round.
P	bird of passage. Migrates and breeds mostly in the tropics. May stay for a short time but does not remain.
III-VI	Breeds from March to June. The figures show the months of the breeding season, the season during which the birds should not be disturbed and the nests should not be approached or touched.
DPL	Display or breeding plumage. This is usually the summer plumage also (SPL). The ducks have this plumage in the winter, sometimes as early as December. The Cormorant develops the DPL early as well and has the duller WPL for only a short time.
WPL	Winter plumage, less striking than the DPL.

1. **Willow Titmouse**—*Parus montanus*
   Head sooty-black. Back dark brown with rufous tinge.
   Wings dark brown with light markings. Breast light red-
   brown with a black fleck on the throat. Nests in holes in
   rotten trees, or sometimes in nesting boxes. Local. **R.
   IV-VI.**

   British Marsh Titmouse—*Parus palustris dresseri Stejn.*
   Well distributed in England. Head glossy blue-black, cheeks
   white; back sandy-brown with an olive tinge; rump browner.
   Wings and tail greyish. Nests in holes in the ground and in
   rotten trees. **R. IV-VI.**

2. **Bearded Titmouse**—*Panurus biarmicus (L.)*
   Head grey-blue. Back tawny-brown; wings brown with
   grey edges; breast white with a pink tinge. There are black
   bearded feathers at the corners of the mouth. The ♀ has a
   brown head and is not bearded. Confined to the Norfolk
   Broads and Devon. **R. IV-VIII.**

3. **Kingfisher**—*Alcedo atthis ispida L.*
   Back blue-green; underparts chestnut brown, having a
   similar patch by the eyes. Chin and neck are white. Red legs.
   Abundant in some districts. Nests in the banks. **R. IV-VI.**

4. **White-spotted Bluethroat**—*Cyanosylvia svecica cyanecula*
   Head and back brown with white streaks above the eyes.
   Underparts a dirty-yellow with a blue patch on the chin and
   the upper part of the breast. In the middle of the blue patch
   is a white spot. There is a red-brown band below the blue.
   Tail black with red-brown at the sides. Rare. Sometimes seen
   on spring migration. **P.**

   Red-spotted Bluethroat—*Cyanosylvia svecica svecica*
   As the previous one with a chestnut-red spot on the blue
   patch. Frequent bird of passage in autumn near the east
   coast. **P.** *(Luscinia svecica)*

5. **Reed Bunting**—*Emberiza schoeniclus (L.)*
DPL: ♂ head and chin black with white collar and white streaks by the corners of the mouth. Back and wings red-brown with black flecks. Underparts dirty-white. ♀ head brown with light-coloured "eyebrow" markings. Chin cinnamon-coloured. In both the ♂ and ♀ the outermost tail feathers are white.
WPL: ♂ has no black on the head and is more like the ♀ in DPL. Fairly common. **R. V-VII.**

6. **Great Reed Warbler**—*Acrocephalus arundinaceus (L.)*
Back olive-brown; underparts brown-grey. "Eyebrow" markings, cheeks and throat white. Has been recorded on migration.

7. **Reed Warbler**—*Acrocephalus scirpaceus (Herm.)*
Back brown; wings darker brown; underparts ash-grey. Head grey-brown with somewhat yellow "eyebrow" markings. Legs dark brown (see no. 9). Common. Nests in reed-beds between the stems. **S. V-VII.**

8. **Savi's Warbler**—*Locustella luscinioides (Savi)*
Back rust-coloured; underparts dirty-white. Tail brown with darker cross streaks. Rare. Sometimes seen in the Fens.

9. **Marsh Warbler**—*Acrocephalus palustris (Becht.)*
Back olive-brown; underparts somewhat yellowish. Cheeks light grey-brown. Legs pale, flesh-coloured. Distinguishable from the Reed Warbler (no. 7) by the greenish colour. Local in some southern countries of England. **VI-VII.**

10. **Grasshopper Warbler**—*Locustella naevia (Bodd.)*
Back brownish-green with darker flecks; underparts dirty-white with a light rusty-brown haze. Wings and tail brown with light edges. Not in extreme north of British Isles. **S. V-VI.**

PLATE XXIX **Birds**

1. Willow Titmouse; 2. Bearded Titmouse; 3. White-spotted Bluethroat;
5. Reed Bunting; 6. Great Reed Warbler; 7. Reed Warbler; 8. Savi's Warbler; 9. Marsh
Warbler; 10. Grasshopper Warbler; 11. Sedge Warbler; 12. Aquatic Warbler.

11. **Sedge Warbler**—*Acrocephalus schoenobaenus (L.)*
Back olive-brown, brown wings with light bands, under-parts dirty-white. Distinguished by white "eyebrow" markings. Fairly common as a summer resident. **VI-VII.**

12. **Aquatic Warbler**—*Acrocephalus paludicola (Vieill.)*
Back brownish-yellow with black flecks and yellowish edges to the feathers. Underparts dirty-white. On the head is a yellowish-white stripe, bounded by broad black stripes, and there are light "eyebrow" markings. Very rare, pro-bably only seen on passage.

13. **Blue-headed Wagtail**—*Motacilla flava L.*
DPL: Back olive-brown, underparts yellow with a white chin. Upper part of the head blue-grey, cheeks black, light "eyebrow" markings. In the winter (**WPL**) the crown and eye-stripes become darker and the underparts paler yellow. Visits Britain regularly and breeds in some places. **V-VII.**

Yellow Wagtail—*Motacilla flava flavissima Blyth.*
Closely resembles the previous bird but the chin is never white and the general appearance is more yellow. **S.**

14. **Pied Wagtail**—*Motacilla alba L.*
DPL: Back blue-grey, underparts and forehead white. Crown and cheek feathers black. Wings dark brown with white bands. Tail black with white edges. Very common. **R. IV-VII.**

Grey Wagtail—*Motacilla cinerea Tun.*
Seen on streams and rivers. Smaller than the previous one but with a longer tail. Slate-blue head and back, greenish rump and tail. Bright yellow underparts. **R. IV-VII.**

15. **Starling**—*Sturnus vulgaris L.*
DPL: Black with a metallic, iridescent sheen and light brown edges to the wing and tail feathers.

WPL: Browner with white edges to all the feathers giving a more speckled appearance. Very common. **R. IV-VII.**

British Dipper—*Cinclus cinclus gularis (Latham)*
Head umber-brown, back slate-grey speckled, with black throat and upper breast white; lower breast chestnut. Belly black. Wings, tail and legs brown. On rapid streams, mostly in the hills, often seen perched on stones, bobbing up and down, hence the name. **R. III-VI.**

16. **Swallow**—*Hirundo rustica L.*
    Back steel-blue, underparts white with a rust-red patch on throat. Forehead and cheeks rust-red also. Tail deeply forked. Long, narrow wings. Catches insects while flying. Common. Nests in barns, under bridges etc. **S. V-VIII**

17. **House Martin**—*Delichon urbica (L.)*
    Back blue-black with a white rump, underparts white. Tail is less deeply forked. Catches insects while flying. Common. Hemi-spherical nests, built on houses etc. **S. V-VII.**

18. **Sand Martin**—*Riparia riparia (L.)*
    Back brown, underparts dirty-white with a brown breast band. Tail slightly forked. Catches insects in flight. Locally common. Nests in steep banks etc., the nest burrow may be up to a yard deep. **V-VII.**

19. **Swift**—*Apus apus (L.)*
    Back brown-black, underparts rather lighter. Wings long, sickle-shaped. Can be seen at twilight, flying high in search of insects. Common. Nests in crevices in walls, cliffs etc. **V-VI or VII.**

20. **Lapwing**—*Vanellus vanellus (L.)*
    Back a shiny green, underparts white with black throat and forehead. Crown of the head black with a metallic sheen,

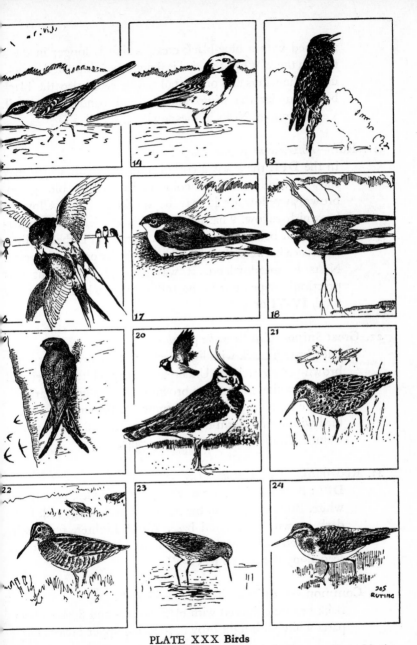

PLATE XXX **Birds**

13. Blue-headed Wagtail; 14. Pied Wagtail; 15. Starling; 16. Swallow; 17. House Martin;
18. Sand Martin; 19. Swift; 20. Lapwing; 21. Ruff; 22. Great Snipe; 23. Redshank;
24. Common Sandpiper.

adorned with a blue-black crest, which is longer in the ♂ than in the ♀. When the bird is flying, the white on the back, under the wings and on the tail can be seen, also the black border under the wings and the end band on the tail. Very common. Nests in meadowland. **R. III-VI.**

21. **Ruff**—*Philomachus pugnax (L.)*
In the **DPL** the ♂ has a conspicuous neck ruff which may show a wide variety of colours, i.e. white, blue-green, brownish-yellow or it may be speckled. Legs yellow or brownish-yellow. ♀ has no ruff and is smaller, the dominating colour being brownish-black. In the **WPL** there is little difference between the ♂ and the ♀. Regular passage migrant. Nests in meadowland. It was once abundant but was practically wiped out in the 19th century when caught for food. **IV-VI or VII.**

22. **Great Snipe**—*Capella media (Lath.)*
Back brown-black with light flecks. On the head are 4 long, brown-yellow stripes. Underparts dirty-white. Outer tail feathers white, the rest are brown with criss-cross marks.
Passage migrant, mostly in autumn. In Britain it is a silent bird without an alarm note. Flies heavily and straight. The Common Snipe (no. 35) flies in zig-zags.

23. **Redshank**—*Tringa totanus (L.)*
DPL: Back greyish-brown with white speckles, underparts white. Brown marks on the head and neck. Legs red. Beak dark brown, with a red base. **WPL:** Lighter, few flecks and no red on the beak. A very noisy bird. Common, often seen along the coasts. **R. IV-VI.**

24. **Common Sandpiper**—*Tringa hypoleucos L.*
Back bronze-coloured with black streaks and flecks, underparts white with light brown, speckled upper breast. Large

primaries are brown-black. Wings have a white edge
Common in the north. **S.**

25. **Black-tailed Godwit**—*Limosa limosa (L.)*
    DPL: Back rusty-brown with black-brown flecks. Rump
    white. Neck and breast red-brown, on the breast are black-
    brown speckles. Underparts white. Can be recognised in
    flight by the white band on the wing and the white rump.
    WPL: Back brown-grey, neck and breast light-grey. Very
    rare. **IV-VI.**

26. **Curlew**—*Numenius arquata (L.)*
    DPL: On the back the feathers are brown-grey with white
    cross streaks, tail lighter, rump white, underparts white
    with brown-grey streaks, the neck is yellowish. Long, down-
    wardly curved beak. ♀ larger and lighter coloured than the ♂.
    Common in many places. In the spring on the moors and
    hills. Abounds on the coasts. **S. IV-VI.**

27. **Black-winged Stilt**—*Himantopus himantopus (L.)*
    White with black shoulders and wings. Black beak. Legs
    long and red. Occurs occasionally on migration.

28. **Herring Gull**—*Larus argentatus Pont.*
    Mantle and wing feathers blue-grey, the ends of the pri-
    maries are black with white tips. Body very white. Large
    yellow beak with a red fleck. Eyes light-yellow. Legs pink.
    In **WPL** small brown-grey streaks over the white feathers.
    Common. Breeds in colonies in dunes. **R. V-VII.**
    The young birds are brownish and speckled. In the 1st.
    year they are dark brown; 2nd, year lighter, with some sil-
    ver-grey feathers on the back; 3rd. year the mantle is silver-
    grey, but the primaries still brown; the 4th. year full-grown.
    The tail-margin in the young bird is brown-black, in the
    adult bird it is white.

29. Black-headed Gull—*Larus ridibundus L.*

Mantle and wings light grey. Primaries white with black tips. Body white. Legs and beak red. In **SPL** it has a brown-black head. **WPL**: There only remain small dark flecks on the ear-coverts and near the eyes. Young are dappled brown. Common. **R. IV-VII.** Breeds on dunes and boglands in large colonies.

30. Common Tern—*Sterna hirundo L.*

SPL: Mantle and wings blue-grey, large primaries darker. Black cap on the head; the rest white. Beak red with a black tip. **WPL**: Forehead white, upperparts black speckled and the rest brown-black. Common. Nests along the coast. Hovers and then dives on to its prey. Catches fish and insects while flying. **S. V-VII.**

31. Black Tern—*Chlidonias niger (L.)*

SPL: Back blue-grey underparts slate-coloured. Head, neck and breast blue-black. Beak black. Dark red-brown legs. **WPL**: Usually lighter. Forehead and belly white. Known as a passage migrant. Catches insects in flight.

32. Water Rail—*Rallus aquaticus L.*

Back dark with brown margins to the feathers. Underparts grey-brown. Flanks and underside of tail black with white cross streaks. Beak dull red, rather curved. Present at all seasons. **IV-VI.**

33. Moorhen or Water Hen—*Gallinula chloropus (L.)*

Back bronze-coloured, belly brown-grey. On the flanks are broad white streaks. Red blaze. Legs green with red bands. Common. **R. IV-VI.**

34. Coot—*Fulica atra L.*

Grey-black with white blaze on the head. Beak white. Common. Nests in reeds on the water. **R. IV-VI or VII.**

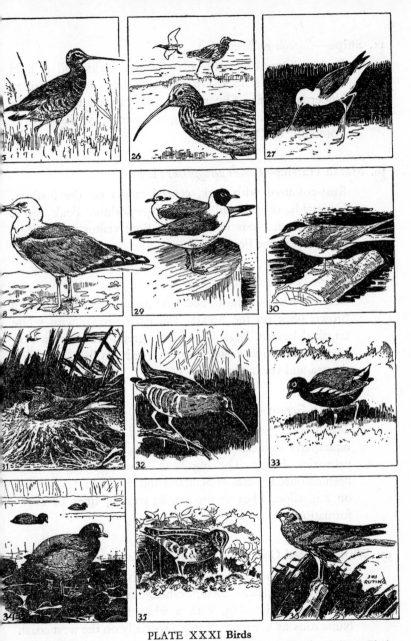

PLATE XXXI Birds

25. Black-tailed Godwit; 26. Curlew; 27. Black-winged Stilt; 28. Herring Gull; 29. Black-headed Gull; 30. Common Tern; 31. Black Tern; 32. Water Rail; 33. Moorhen; 34. Coot; 35. Snipe; 36. Marsh Harrier.

35. Snipe—*Capella gallinago (L.)*

Back brown-black with rusty-brown flecks and 4 light brown-yellow stripes. On the head are 3 similar stripes. Underparts white. Outermost tail feathers white-edged, the rest rust-brown with black zig-zag markings. (See no. 22). Common. **R. IV-VIII.**

36. Marsh Harrier—*Circus aeruginosus (L.)*

Rust-coloured with dark, central marks on the feathers. Underside of the tail feathers grey-white. Beak black. Legs yellow. Nests in the reeds. Rare visitor on passage, some nest in the Fens. **V-VI.**

37. Osprey—*Pandion haliaetus (L.)*

Beak dark brown; head, neck and underparts white, with a brown fleck on the breast. Tail dark brown with white terminal border. Beak black. Legs green-grey. Known on passage, inland and on the coast. Feeds on fish from both the sea and fresh water.

38. Grey Lag Goose—*Anser anser (L.)*

The largest goose. Head, neck and back brown-grey; underparts lighter. Wing feathers are greyish-brown, the primaries darker. The big beak is orange-yellow. Legs flesh-coloured. Nests in Scotland and the Hebrides, known on migration. Flies in groups, in straight lines or in V-formation.

39. White-fronted Goose—*Anser albifrons (Scop.)*

Smaller than no. 38 and browner. On the back are large black blotches. Beak small, flesh-coloured, round the base of it is a white ring, with a white mark on the head. Numerous as a winter visitor, especially on the west coast.

40. Bean Goose—*Anser fabalis (Lath.)*

Back dark brown. Underparts grey-brown, without black marks. Head and neck chestnut brown. Beak black with an orange band. Legs orange. Uncommon winter visitor. Locally numerous.

Pink-footed Goose—*Anser brachyrhynchus Baill.*
Like no. 40 but smaller. Head and neck darker brown. Beak black with a pink band. Legs pink. Well known as a winter visitor.

41. Whooper Swan—*Cygnus cygnus (L.)*

Completely white. Beak black. On the head is a wedge-shaped yellow patch, continuing over the top of the beak. In the young birds this mark is pinkish-grey and the head, neck and wings are brownish-grey. Common. **W.**

Bewick's Swan—*Cygnus bewickii Yarr.*
Smaller than the previous one. The yellow mark does not go over the top of the beak, which is completely black. Common as a winter visitor, especially in Scotland.

41a. Mute Swan—*Cygnus olor (Gm.)*

Beak and wedge-shaped patch are orange-red. Black knob on the forehead. Base, edge and tip of the lower beak are black. Common but usually semi-domesticated. **R.**

42. Gadwall—*Anas strepera L.*

DPL: ♂ body brown-grey, the upperparts darker with light and dark cross markings. Wings are also brown-grey with light and dark cross marks and a brown and a black band before a white mirror. ♀ completely yellow-brown with darker flecks on the wings and a brown and a grey stripe before a small white mirror. In **SPL** the ♂ is more like the ♀. Rare. Breeds in East Anglia and in Scotland. **R and W.**

43. **Teal**—*Anas crecca L.*

Small duck. **DPL:** ♂ has back, primaries and tail brown-grey. Underparts white with round black spots. Head and neck cinammon-red. Round the eye is a green patch with a yellow-white border. Wings grey with greeny-black mirrors, the front edge is yellow-white and there is a small, white margin at the back. ♀ completely grey-brown with speckles. Wing-mirrors as in the ♂. Fairly common, especially in the north. **R. IV-VI.**

(*Querquedula crecca*)

44. **Garganey**—*Anas querquedula L.*

Similar in size to no. 43. **DPL:** ♂ head and breast brown with white "eyebrow" markings, extending down the neck. Back dark brown, underparts greyish-white. Wings grey, having green mirrors with distinct white edges. ♀ like the ♀ of the Mallard (no. 47), but with faint "eyebrow" markings and, on the grey wing, a duller mirror than in the ♂. Numerous as summer visitor in East Anglia and Kent, rarer in other parts of the British Isles. **IV-VI.**

(*Querquedula querquedula*)

45. **Shoveler**—*Spatula clypeata (L.)*

DPL: ♂ back brown-black with white shoulders. Head green, beak spoon-shaped and broad. Back chestnut-brown with a white breast. Wings grey, light-blue at the front. Green mirror with a white border. ♀ brown with yellow edges to the feathers and darker flecks, the front edges of the wings blue-grey.

Fairly common as a passage migrant and winter visitor. Some resident.

46. **Pochard**—*Aythya ferina (L.)*

DPL: ♂ back, flanks and wings grey, the brown-black on the breast continues in a band over the back. Head and neck reddish-brown. Underparts whitish-grey, becoming black

PLATE XXXII **Birds**

37. Osprey; 38. Grey Lag Goose; 39. White-fronted Goose; 40. Bean Goose; 41. Whooper
Swan; 41a. Mute Swan; 42. Gadwall; 43. Teal; 44. Garganey; 45. Shoveler; 46. Pochard;
47. Mallard; 48. Tufted Duck.

towards the breast. ♀ brown-grey, speckled; cheeks and neck reddish-brown. Many resident. Very numerous in winter. *(Nyroca ferina)*

47. **Mallard**—*Anas platyrhyncha L.*

   DPL: ♂ head green, a white ring round the neck. Back dark brown; underparts grey with dark brown breast and black belly. Wings grey with blue mirrors edged with white. Tail feathers are upcurled. ♀ brownish-yellow, with darker flecks and blue mirrors. Very common. Resident and abundant as a migrant. **III-V.**

   Widgeon—*Mareca penelope (L.)*

   DPL: ♂ head rust-brown, forehead yellow. Back grey, underparts white with a red-brown breast and black under the tail. Wings white at the front becoming grey with green mirrors. ♀ rather like the ♀ Mallard but the back is darker, underparts white and the flanks, head and neck are reddish-brown.

   SPL: ♂ like the DPL but with a brown-grey haze and speckling. Common winter visitor. Nests in north Scotland.

48. **Tufted Duck**—*Aythya fuligula (L.)*

   DPL: ♂ belly and flanks white, becoming black. A long crest on the head. White wing stripes. ♀ brown-grey with dark brown throat, head and crest. A white wing stripe. Is becoming commoner and is resident all over the British Isles. *(Nyroca fuligula)*

49. **Scaup Duck**—*Aythya marila (L.)*

   DPL: ♂ head, neck, breast and part of the tail black, back grey. Underparts and flanks white. Wings grey with a white stripe. ♀ head and throat dark brown, sometimes with a white spot round the base of the beak. Breast and part of the tail grey-brown, flanks grey. Wings brown with white wing streaks.

   A winter visitor, often abundant but rare inland.

50. Goosander—*Mergus merganser* L.

♂ head, neck and back black with a green sheen, underparts salmon-coloured. Beak red, long and narrow, with a serrated edge. Legs red. A very short crest.

♀ chestnut-brown head with a large crest. Throat white. Back grey, underparts white. A regular visitor to the inland waters of Scotland and north England. Elsewhere a more casual visitor, mostly in the winter.

51. Merganser—*Mergus serrator* L.

♂ with long crest on the black head, with a white neck ring. Back black with a green sheen. Belly white, breast brown. Wing black with a large, square, white patch, having two white stripes. ♀ with a brown head and a somewhat smaller crest. Breast light grey, speckled. Common resident in parts of Scotland and Ireland. A winter visitor in England and Wales.

52. Smew—*Mergellus albellus* (L.)

♂ almost white, except for a fleck near the eye, a stripe on both sides of the back of the head, a band over the back and small streaks on the breast, all of which are black. The primaries are brownish-black and the tail grey. On the head is a short crest. ♀ has dark grey back. Head with short crest which is brown like the throat. Underparts dirty-white. Occurs occasionally in all parts of Britain, mostly as a winter visitor.

53. Cormorant—*Phalocrocorax carbo* (L.)

DPL: black with a brownish-green sheen, the wings are also brown-green. Behind the eye is a patch of naked, yellow skin. Small white feathers on the head and neck, and there is a white fleck on the thigh. **WPL:** no white feathers on the head or thighs. Breeds in large colonies on rocky coasts but is also found on inland waters. A fish-eater.

Dives well. When the bird is swimming only the back and throat can be seen. **R. III-VII.**

54. **Heron**—*Ardea cinerea L.*

> **DPL**: Back blue-grey. underparts white. Blue-black display feathers on the back of the head. Breast white. A broad black stripe near the eye. Beak is orange-yellow with a darker tip.
>
> **WPL**: Almost the same, the beak flesh-coloured. Common. **R. II-VI.** Breeds in colonies in trees. Flies with curved neck, the legs extended backwards.

55. **Little Bittern**—*Ixobrychus minutus (L.)*

> ♂ back black, underparts brown-yellow with darker streaks. Wings black and yellow. ♀ lighter coloured, where the ♂ is black the ♀ is brown. An irregular visitor on migration. May nest in Norfolk.

56. **Bittern**—*Botaurus stellaris (L.)*

> Brownish-yellow with darker and lighter edges to the feathers, stripes and flecks. Back darker than the belly, throat white. Spring and autumn migrant and winter visitor. Principally a night bird, hides in the reeds during the day.

57. **White Stork**—*Ciconia ciconia (L.)*

> White, usually with black on the wings. Beak and legs red. Flies with outstretched neck. A rare visitor on passage.

58. **Spoonbill**—*Platalea leucorodia L.*

> White, yellow tinge on the throat and the crest. Beak spoon-shaped, black with yellow bands. Legs black.
> A regular visitor to East Anglia, rare elsewhere.

PLATE XXXIII **Birds**

49. Scaup Duck; 50. Goosander; 51. Merganser; 52. Smew; 53. Cormorant; 54. Heron;
55. Little Bittern; 56. Bittern; 57. White Stork; 58. Spoonbill; 59. Dabchick; 60. Great
Crested Grebe.

59. Dabchick or Little Grebe—*Podiceps ruficollis (Pall.)*

DPL: Back dark brown, underparts brownish-grey. The sides of the head and the neck red-brown. Less distinct in the ♀.

WPL: The red-brown on the head and neck is absent. Underparts light grey, almost white. A common resident in most parts of the British Isles. Makes a nest of reeds, usually floating. In the winter is often found on the coast. **IV-VIII.**

60. Great Crested Grebe—*Podiceps cristatus (L.)*

Back brownish-black, underparts dirty-white. In the **DPL** there is a long, black crest on the head and a red-brown neck-collar, with a black edging. The collar of the ♂ is more distinct than that of the ♀. Beak red. Common over most of the British Isles. A good diver. **R. V-VII.**

Black-necked Grebe—*Podiceps nigricollis Brehm*
DPL: Back, neck and upper part of the breast black. Behind the eye are long yellow-brown feathers. Belly white, flanks red-brown. Beak dull, uptilted. Mostly known as a passage migrant.

MAMMALS *(Mammalia)*

Of all the mammals which exist, only a few are mentioned in this book. They belong to three different orders, namely the Insectivores (no. 1), the Rodents (nos. 2 to 5) and the Carnivores (no. 6).

There are many mammals which are known to visit the water's edge, for nearly all mammals drink water and must consequently go occasionally to a pond or stream to obtain it. Cows, horses, sheep etc. have not been described here, but only the animals which live by the water and find their food there.

The length of the body and that of the tail are recorded separately.

1. **Water Shrew**—*Neomys fodiens (Schr.)*

Dark, velvety fur, slate-grey to black. Has a pointed snout. The upper lip and nose protrude further than the under lip. Belly light grey. Has stiff, bristle-like hairs on the tail. It can remain under water for a long time. Has its burrow with one entrance under water and one above.
Food: snails; beetles; fish, especially carp; small birds; tadpoles etc.
Not common, mostly found in clear streams.
$2\frac{1}{2}$ + 2 inches.

2. **Continental Field Vole**—*Microtus arvalis (Pall.)*

Back and sides grey-brown; belly dirty-white. Small ears; short, stout, hairy tail. Damages crops. 4 + 1 inch.
Not found in Great Britain.

3. **Water Vole or Water Rat**—*Arvicola amphibius (L.)*

Dark brown with short, blunt head. Short, strong, hairy tail. Can do much damage by making holes in the banks and in dams. Herbivorous; eats roots and the bark of trees, particularly willows.
Very common. 6 + 3 inches.

Musk Rat—*Ondatra zibethica L.*
Introduced between 1927 and 1932. Practically exterminated. Has a laterally compressed tail, almost as long as the body. Does serious damage to dams. Food: grain; potatoes etc. 14 + 10 inches. *(Fiber zibethicus)*

4. **Harvest Mouse**—*Micromys minutus soricinus (Herm.)*

Back red-brown; belly dirty-white. Makes a globular nest in corn and sometimes among reeds.
Common. 3 + $2\frac{1}{2}$ inches.

5. **Brown Rat**—R*attus norvegicus (Berk.)*

> Blunt head, short hairy ears. Short legs. Thick, strong, scaly tail. Grey-brown, though the colour varies.
> Common along water courses, sewers, drains etc. Omnivorous. 5 + 4 inches.
> (*Epimys norvegicus*)

6. **Otter**—L*utra lutra (L.)*

> Glossy, dark-brown coat, lighter on the cheeks and the belly. The hairs do not get wet. Webbed toes. Small ear-lobes, which can be closed when the animal dives. The nostrils can also be closed. Catches large numbers of fish by diving under water. Rather rare and timid. Is often hunted. Found in large pools and broad water-courses. 2-3 feet + 1½ feet.

PLATE XXXIV **Mammals**
1. Water Shrew; 2. Continental Field Vole; 3. Water Vole; 4. Harvest Mouse; 5. Brown Rat;
6. Otter.

BOOKS FOR FURTHER READING

T. T. Macan and E. B. Worthington. LIFE IN LAKES AND RIVERS. *Collins.*
K. E. Carpenter. LIFE IN INLAND WATERS. *Sidgwick & Jackson.*
W. S. Furneaux. LIFE IN PONDS AND STREAMS. *Longmans.*
J. G. Needham and J. T. Lloyd. LIFE OF INLAND WATERS. *Comstock & Constable.*
J. Clegg. FRESHWATER LIFE OF THE BRITISH ISLES. *Warne.*
J. Clegg. POND LIFE. *Warne (Observer Series).*
G. C. Bateman. FRESHWATER AQUARIA. *Link House.*
W. T. Garnett. FRESHWATER MICROSCOPY. *Constable.*
J. G. and P. R. Needham. FRESHWATER BIOLOGY. *Constable.*
E. J. Popham. SOME ASPECTS OF LIFE IN FRESHWATER. *Heinemann.*
J. Clegg (Ed.) POND AND STREAM LIFE OF EUROPE. *Blandford.*
W. Engelhardt. THE YOUNG SPECIALIST LOOKS AT POND LIFE. *Burke.*
W. B. Ward and G. C. Whipple. FRESHWATER BIOLOGY. *Wiley.*

Clapham, Tutin and Warburg. FLORA OF THE BRITISH ISLES. *Cambridge.*
D. McClintock and R. S. R. Fitter. POCKET GUIDE TO WILD FLOWERS. *Collins.*
Bentham and Hooker. HANDBOOK OF BRITISH FLORA. *Reeve.*
W. H. Fitch and W. G. Smith. ILLUSTRATIONS TO THE BRITISH FLORA. *Reeve.*
R. W. Butcher and F. E. Strudwick. FURTHER ILLUSTRATIONS. *Reeve.*
L. J. F. Brimble. FLORAL YEAR. *Macmillan.*
W. J. Stokoe. BRITISH GRASSES, SEDGES AND RUSHES. *Warne.*
E. Step. BRITISH WILD FLOWERS. *Warne (Observer Series).*
W. Keble Martin. THE CONCISE BRITISH FLORA IN COLOUR. *Michael Joseph.*

F. H. Brightman and B. E. Nicholson. OXFORD BOOK OF FLOWERLESS PLANTS. *Oxford.*
P. G. Taylor. BRITISH FERNS AND MOSSES (The Kew Series). *Eyre & Spottiswoode.*

G. S. West and F. E. Fritsch. BRITISH FRESHWATER ALGAE. *Cambridge.*

R. Buchsbaum. ANIMALS WITHOUT BACKBONES. *Pelican (2 vols).*
H. Mellanby. ANIMAL LIFE IN FRESH WATER. *Methuen.*
T. T. Macan. GUIDE TO FRESHWATER INVERTEBRATE ANIMALS. *Longmans.*

E. Step. SHELL LIFE. *Warne.*
P. Welch. LIMNOLOGY. *McGraw Hill.*
H. Janus. THE YOUNG SPECIALIST LOOKS AT MOLLUSCS. *Burke.*

C. Longfield. DRAGONFLIES OF THE BRITISH ISLES. *Warne.*
N. H. Joy. HANDBOOK OF BRITISH BEETLES. *Warne.*
F. Balfour-Browne. BRITISH WATER BEETLES. *Ray Society.*
J. R. Dibb. FIELD BOOK OF BEETLES.
G. H. Verrall. BRITISH FLIES.

C. N. Colyer and C. O. Hammond. FLIES OF THE BRITISH ISLES. *Warne.*
E. Step. BEES, WASPS, ANTS AND ALLIED INSECTS. *Warne.*
R. South. BUTTERFLIES OF THE BRITISH ISLES. *Warne.*
R. South. MOTHS OF THE BRITISH ISLES. *Warne. (2 vo s.)*
W. J. Stokoe. BRITISH BUTTERFLIES. *Warne (Observer Series).*
M. Burr. BRITISH GRASSHOPPERS.
M. E. Moseley. BRITISH CADDIS FLIES. *Routledge.*
N. E. Hickin. CADDIS. *Methuen.*
A. D. Imms. INSECT NATURAL HISTORY. *Co lins.*
N. D. Riley (Ed.) INSECTS IN COLOUR. *Blandford.*

J. T. Jenkins. FISHES OF THE BRITISH ISLES. *Warne.*
A. L. Wells. FRESHWATER FISHES OF THE BRITISH ISLES. *Warne (Observer Series).*
A. J. Taylor. FISH OF RIVERS, LAKES AND PONDS. *Blandford.*

M. Smith. THE BRITISH AMPHIBIA AND REPTILES. *Collins.*
L. H. Matthews. THE BRITISH AMPHIBIA AND REPTILES. *Methuen.*
Maxwell Knight. FROGS, TOADS AND NEWTS IN BRITAIN. *Brockhampton Press.*
A. Leutscher (Ed.) REPTILES AND AMPHIBIANS. *Burke.*

P. A. D. Hollom. THE POPULAR HANDBOOK OF BRITISH BIRDS. *Witherby.*
T. A. Coward. BIRDS OF THE BRITISH ISLES. *Warne.*
H. Witherby. HANDBOOK OF BRITISH BIRDS. *Witherby.*
R. S. R. Fitter and J. H. A. Richardson. POCKET GUIDE TO BRITISH BIRDS. *Collins.*
A. Frieling. THE YOUNG SPECIALIST LOOKS AT BIRDS. *Burke.*
R. T. Peterson, G. Mountfort and P. A. D. Hollom. A FIELD GUIDE TO THE BIRDS OF BRITAIN AND EUROPE. *Collins.*

W. J. Stokoe. WILD ANIMALS OF THE BRITISH ISLES. *Warne.*
O. G. Pike. WILD ANIMALS OF BRITAIN. *Macmillan.*
E. Step. ANIMAL LIFE OF THE BRITISH ISLES. *Warne.*
L. H. Matthews. BRITISH MAMMALS. *Collins.*
Stehli and Brohmer (translated by A. Leutscher). THE YOUNG SPECIALIST LOOKS AT MAMMALS. *Burke.*

THE SCIENTIFIC PUBLICATIONS OF THE FRESHWATER BIOLOGICAL ASSOCIATION.

GLOSSARY

♂ ..... male   ♀ ..... female

ACCESSORY, additional.
AMPHIDISC, see page 49.
ANIMALCULE, microscopic animal.
ANTENNA, feeler.
ANTERIOR, in front.
ANUS, terminal opening of intestine.
APPENDAGE, limb or other outgrowth of body.
AXIS, main stem.

BARBEL, beard-like projection in some fish.
BASAL, bottom.
BILOBED, in two portions.
BIVALVE, mollusc with two shells.
BLAZE (in birds), patch of coloured feathers on the head.
BRACKISH, water containing a small amount of salt.
BRACT, leaf-like outgrowth on a flower stem.
BULBOUS, swollen.
BYSSUS, sticky threads for attachment.

CALCAREOUS, containing lime, chalky.
CALYX, sepal-cup of a flower.
CAPITULUM, 'flower' (e.g. Daisy) formed of small, sessile florets massed together.
CARAPACE, dorsal 'shell' of crabs etc.
CARNIVORE, flesh eating animal.
CEPHALO-THORAX, carapace of both head and thorax fused into one piece.
CHITIN, horny material.
CHLOROPHYLL, green pigment in leaves.
CHLOROPLAST, structure containing chlorophyll in a cell.
CILIA, small protoplasmic projections.
COLUMELLA (in molluscs), central axis of shell.
COMPRESSED, flattened.

CONCHINE, horny, organic material.
CONCAVE, hollowed.
CONVEX, domed.
CORDATE, heart-shaped.
COROLLA, petals of a flower.
CORYMB, raceme with flowers on one level, the outer ones having longer stalks.
CYME, inflorescence in which the main axis ends in a flower and younger flowers are on the side branches.

DECURRENT, growing down on to the stem
DETRITUS, organic waste.
DIAMETER, the distance across.
DICHOTOMOUS, forked branching.
DISC-FLORETS, central, small flowers in many capitula.
DIVERGENT, spreading.
DORSAL, back or outer part.

EMARGINATED, shallowly notched at the tip.
ENCRUSTATION, a rough covering.
ENTIRE (eg. leaf-margin), unbroken.
EPIDERMIS, outer layer of cells.
EXCURRENT, growing towards the top of the stem.
EXO-SKELETON, outer 'shell' of some lower animals.

FILAMENT, thread; stem of stamen.
FLACCID, weak, limp.
FLAGELLUM, whip-like thread.
FLORET, small flower.
FRUCTIFICATION, formation of a fruit.

GAMETE, reproductive cell.
GEMMULE, reproductive mass in sponges.

GILL, breathing organ in some water animals.

GLOBOSE, spherical.

GONOPHORE, reproductive individual in coelenterates.

HAEMOGLOBIN, red colour in blood.

HYBRID, the result of crossing different varieties.

HYDROID, feeding animal in many coelenterates.

INDENTED, notched.

INFLORESCENCE, stem bearing several flowers.

INORGANIC, not living.

INSECTIVORE, animal which eats insects.

INVOLUCRE, cup-shaped mass of bracts.

IRIDESCENT, coloured like a rainbow.

LANCEOLATE, long and narrow, broadest in the middle.

LARVA, immature, independent stage of an animal, unlike the adult.

LEAF-AXIL, angle between the leaf-stalk and the main stem.

LEAFLET, portion of a compound leaf.

LIGAMENT, binding tissue.

LINEAR, narrow, sides almost parallel.

LIVE-BEARER, animal which produces living young without laying eggs.

LIVERWORT, simple, non-flowering plant, related to the mosses.

LOPHOPHORE, see page 58.

MANTLE, outer layer. Dorsal feathers in a bird.

MEMBRANOUS, thin and papery.

MESOTHORAX, second segment of the thorax.

METAMORPHOSIS, change in form from the larva to the adult.

MID-RIB, central vein of a leaf.

MIRROR (in birds), patch, often white, on the wing feathers.

MOTILE, capable of movement.

MUCUS, slimy secretion.

NAUPLIUS, larval stage of some crustaceans.

NECTARY, honey-bag.

NODE, knob; place at which a leaf is attached to a stem.

NODULE, small knob.

OBOVATE, oval, broadest at the top.

OBTUSE, blunt.

OPAQUE, solid: not transparent.

OPERCULUM, lid.

ORGANIC, living or once living.

OSCULUM, opening in a sponge.

OVATE, oval, broadest at the bottom.

OVIPAROUS, lays eggs.

OVIPOSITOR, organ for laying eggs.

OVIVIPAROUS, eggs retained inside the mother until hatched.

PALMATE, hand-shaped.

PALMATI-PARTITE, divided palmately.

PANICLE, compound raceme.

PAPPUS, calyx reduced to hairs.

PARASITE, organism which obtains its food from another without giving any benefit in return.

PEDICEL, flower stalk.

PEDUNCLE, inflorescence axis.

PERFOLIATE, stem passing through the leaf.

PERISTOME, structure round the mouth. See page 58.

PETAL, flower leaf, usually coloured.

PETIOLE, leaf stalk.

PINNATE, divided like a feather.

PISTIL, female part of a flower.

PISTILLATE, containing pistils only; female flower.

PLANKTON, microscopic organisms in surface waters.

PLICATE, folded longways.

POLYP, a hydroid.

POSTERIOR, behind.

PREHENSILE, grasping.

PRIMARIES, main wing feathers of a bird.

PROBOSCIS, sucking mouth or tongue.

PROCUMBENT, lying on the ground.

PROTHORAX, first segment of the thorax.

PUPA, chrysalis; resting stage in an insect during which metamorphosis occurs.

RACEME, inflorescence on a long axis with the youngest flowers at the top.

RADICAL, growing from the ground.

RADULA, tongue of a snail.

RASPING, rough.

RAY-FLORETS, the conspicuous flowers of a capitulum, often only on the outside.

RECTAL GILLS, see page 90.

REGENERATION, reforming of damaged parts.

ROOTLET, small root.

ROOTSTOCK, swollen, underground stem.

ROSETTE, ring of leaves.

ROSTRUM, beak-like projection of a carapace.

SEPAL, outer flower-leaf, usually green.

SESSILE, without a stalk.

SILICA, sandy material.

SILICEOUS, containing silica.

SILIQUA, pod-like fruit with a central wall.

SPADIX, fleshy spike.

SPATULATE, spoon-shaped.

SPERMATOZOA, male gametes.

SPICULE, small, needle-like spine.

SPIKE, raceme with sessile flowers.

SPINOUS, with spines, prickly.

SPIRACLE, breathing hole.

SPONGIN, soft, gelatinous material in sponges.

SPORE, non-sexual reproductive cell, usually thick-walled.

STAMEN, pollen-bearing part of the flower.

STAMINATE, with stamens. Male flower.

STATOBLAST, see page 58.

STATOCYST, balance organ. See page 53.

STIPULES, pair of outgrowths at the base of a leaf.

STOLON, runner.

SUTURE, connecting groove or seam.

TARSUS, 'foot' region of insect leg.

TENTACLE, finger-like outgrowth.

TERNATE, three-lobed.

THALLUS, simple, flattened, plant-body.

THORAX, chest region.

TRACHEA, breathing tube.

TRANSLUCENT, partially transparent.

TRANSPARENT, can be seen through.

TRUNCATED, cut short.

TUBER, swollen, food-storing, underground organ.

TUBERCLE, small swelling.

UMBEL, raceme with flower stalks at the same level.

UMBILICUS, see page 62.

UMBO, apex of bivalve shell.

UNDULATING, wavy.

VALVE, one section of a shell, pod etc.

VENTRAL, lower or inner surface.

VERTEBRATE, animal with an internal skeleton.

VIVIPAROUS, having living young.

WHORL, ring (of leaves etc.).

ZOOSPORE, motile reproductive cell.

INDEX

153

154